IN THE HEIGHTS

The Applause Libretto Library Series

THE COMPLETE BOOK AND LYRICS
OF THE BROADWAY MUSICAL

Music and Lyrics by Lin-Manuel Miranda

Book by Quiara Alegría Hudes

Conceived by Lin-Manuel Miranda

APPLAUSE
THEATRE & CINEMA BOOKS

Published in 2013 by Applause Theatre & Cinema Books
4501 Forbes Blvd., #200
Lanham, Maryland 20706
www.rowman.com

All photos of the original Broadway cast © Joan Marcus

Distributed by NATIONAL BOOK NETWORK

Book design by Mark Lerner

Library of Congress Cataloging-in-Publication Data is available upon request.

ISBN 978-1-4768-7464-7

www.applausebooks.com

In The Heights was originally produced on Broadway by Kevin McCollum, Jeffrey Seller, Jill Furman, Sander Jacobs, Robyn Goodman/Walt Grossman, Peter Fine, and Sonny Everett/ Mike Skipper. The associate producers were Ruth Hendel and Harold Newman.

Development of *In The Heights* was supported by the Eugene O'Neill Theater Center during a residency at the Music Theater Conference of 2005. It was initially developed by Back House Productions. It premiered on Broadway at the Richard Rodgers Theatre on March 9, 2008, and ran for 1,184 performances.

CONTENTS

INTRODUCTION

Lights up on the basement of the Drama Book Shop, a tiny black box theater on West 40th in Manhattan. It's February 24, 2003, and I've been asked to attend a reading of a new musical called In The Heights, composed, written, and starring Lin-Manuel Miranda, an unknown twenty-three-year-old who began writing the piece while a sophomore at Wesleyan. It's being presented by Back House Productions, a small not-for-profit run by four young Wesleyan graduates, one of whom, Thomas Kail, is also the director. I have no idea what to expect, but let's just say I expect very little. And then it begins. Lin bursts onto the stage as Usnavi, and starts rapping about his Washington Heights neighborhood, his bodega, and his community. My mouth fell open. I got goose bumps (and have them even now, as I reminisce). I was mesmerized, transported in a way I always hope to be when I'm watching something new, but rarely am. It was music I had never heard before in a musical, and a method of storytelling that was fresh, unique, exciting, and had energy to burn. I knew immediately I was in the presence of a musical genius and had to be involved with this project.

Soon after I signed on as a producer, I was joined by the prestigious producing team of Kevin McCollum and Jeffrey Seller. We all believed Lin was special and that the material had the potential to be a landmark musical, but that it would require a great deal of work. Lin would readily admit he's not a book writer, so we began trying to find a writer who could make the book sing in the same way the music did. Enter Quiara Hudes, who had recently received an MFA from the playwriting program at Brown University. She and Lin had similar backgrounds, and like the In The Heights character of Nina Rosario, Quiara was the first person in her family to go to college, having received her undergraduate degree in musical composition from Yale. She understood the world and story completely, and also had a real feel for the rhythms of the neighborhood. We knew immediately she was the perfect person to join Lin on this journey.

And so the development process began in earnest. What started as a small love story that happened to be set in the particular area of Washington Heights in upper Manhattan morphed into a love letter to the entire neighborhood and its diverse Latino culture. Like so many seminal musicals that had come before, the piece began to focus on the immigrant experience and chasing the American Dream. Universal themes began to take shape about the notion of home and gentrification—what does home mean to different people, and what happens if the home you've always known begins to change before your eyes? The music became richer and more kaleidoscopic, reflecting Lin's desire that it sound like the tapestry of music he would hear walking from 181st to 191st in the neighborhood, the boleros wafting from apartment windows, the rap blaring from boom boxes strapped to bicycles, the merengue coming from bodegas on the corner.

We worked closely with Tommy Kail, and Alex Lacamoire and Bill Sherman, our co-orchestrators and arrangers. A reading of the new first act was held in December 2004, followed by another reading in April 2005. We went to the O'Neill Musical Theatre Conference in July 2005 and presented a full workshop version in March 2006. Throughout the five-year development process, we went through numerous drafts—in my office I have twenty-four different versions of the script piled on a shelf, and I wouldn't be surprised if I were missing some. Lin wrote at least sixty songs (or versions of songs) that were included at some point in the process but didn't ultimately make it into the final production—they've become "trunk" songs. Lin and Quiara excised characters and added new ones.

The aforementioned workshop in 2006 was a backers' audition—a chance to invite producers, theater owners, and other members of the theatrical community to gauge interest and support as we made the decision whether to move forward with a full production. And once again, as had occurred at every other point in the process, our instincts about the show—that it was moving, exciting, new, and yet somehow familiar—were shared by everyone, and we knew we were on our way to mounting the show.

As we readied our first production, Andy Blankenbuehler was brought on as our choreographer, and he was joined by a superb design team, including Anna Louizos (sets), Paul Tazewell (costumes), Nevin Steinberg (sound), and Howell Binkley (lighting). Our cast, many of whom had been with the show since its earliest incarnations, was equally superlative, and together the team contributed to the magic realized onstage night after night.

We still hoped *In The Heights* would make it to Broadway, but we couldn't bring it straight in. Most new musicals do "out-of-town tryouts" across the country in cities like Los Angeles, Seattle, and Chicago. But because *In The Heights* was a distinctly New York show, we decided to do an "in-town out-of-town tryout" and produced it at 37 Arts, an Off-Broadway theater. Previews began on January

9, 2007, and the show opened on February 8 to positive notices and enthusiastic audience response. When the show closed in July, we were committed to taking the leap and moving to Broadway, but were well aware of what needed to be done. After six months of intensive work, and a handful of new co-producing partners joining the team, we were ready.

The Broadway incarnation of *In The Heights* began previews at the Richard Rodgers Theatre on February 14, 2008, almost five years to the day when I had seen the reading in the basement of the Drama Book Shop, and a little over eight years since Lin first presented the material at his twentieth birthday party in his parents' house in Inwood, the neighborhood just north of Washington Heights where he grew up. There was something fitting about being at the Rodgers, named after one-half of the most celebrated songwriting team in musical theater history, given Lin's affection for classic Broadway musicals and the fact that *In The Heights* owed as much to them as to contemporary hip-hop. After opening on March 9 to overwhelming critical and audience acclaim, the show took Broadway by storm, receiving thirteen Tony nominations and winning the coveted Best Musical award, along with those for Lin's score, Andy's choreography, and Alex and Bill's orchestrations. In addition to numerous other awards and nominations, it also won the Grammy Award for Best Original Cast Recording, and Lin and Quiara were finalists for the Pulitzer Prize for Drama (Quiara went on to win in 2012, after her third time as a finalist). The show ultimately ran on Broadway for 1,184 performances, closing on January 9, 2011, and went out on two national tours.

Helping to foster new work is always satisfying, but I can't imagine a more exhilarating and rewarding experience than being involved with *In The Heights* from such an early stage. Kevin, Jeffrey, and I made a conscious early decision to put our faith in a young and untested creative team, and it paid off in spades. In addition to launching numerous careers, *In The Heights* broke new musical theater ground. While the show was rooted in traditional musical theater storytelling traditions, it helped usher in a new era on Broadway by being the first musical to successfully integrate hip-hop into the aural landscape. It spoke to every demographic and every age group—it was the kind of show a fifteen-year-old could go to with her friend and have one experience, and then take her grandmother to see and have an altogether different one. It depicted Latino culture in a positive and realistic light, whereas the few previous theatrical examples were, unfortunately, more stereotypical and negative. Thousands of Latino kids who had never seen a Broadway show before came to *In The Heights*, saw themselves up on that stage, and realized that their stories were meaningful and worthy of being told too. All involved with *In The Heights* have gone on to conquer new creative challenges, but *In The Heights* was special. It was the first time for so many of us, and we were so proud of everything we and the show had accomplished. The making of *In The Heights* was joyful, rich, rewarding, and full of life, much like the show itself.

—Jill Furman
October 2012

INTRODUCTION

ORIGINAL BROADWAY CAST AND CREDITS

In The Heights
Music and Lyrics by Lin-Manuel Miranda
Book by Quiara Alegría Hudes
Conceived by Lin-Manuel Miranda

USNAVI	Lin-Manuel Miranda
NINA	Mandy Gonzalez
KEVIN	Carlos Gomez
CAMILA	Priscilla Lopez
BENNY	Christopher Jackson
VANESSA	Karen Olivo
SONNY	Robin De Jesús
ABUELA CLAUDIA	Olga Merediz
DANIELA	Andréa Burns
CARLA	Janet Dacal
GRAFFITI PETE	Seth Stewart
PIRAGUA GUY	Eliseo Román
ENSEMBLE	Tony Chiroldes
	Rosie Lani Fiedelman
	Joshua Henry
	Afra Hines
	Nina Lafarga
	Doreen Montalvo
	Javier Muñoz
	Krysta Rodriguez
	Eliseo Román
	Luis Salgado
	Shaun Taylor-Corbett
	Rickey Tripp

Swings: Michael Balderrama, Blanca Camacho, Rogelio Douglas Jr., and Stephanie Klemons

Director: Thomas Kail
Choreographer: Andy Blankenbuehler
Musical Director: Alex Lacamoire
Set Designer: Anna Louizos
Costume Designer: Paul Tazewell
Lighting Designer: Howell Binkley
Sound Designer: Acme Sound Partners
Music Arrangers/Orchestrators: Alex Lacamoire and Bill Sherman
Music Coordinator: Michael Keller
Casting: Telsey & Company
Company Manager: Brig Berney
General Managers: John S. Corker and Lizbeth Cone
Technical Supervisor: Brian Lynch
Production Stage Manager: J. Philip Bassett
Stage Manager: Amber Wedin
Assistant Stage Manager: Heather Hogan

CHARACTERS AND SETTING

CHARACTERS

USNAVI DE LA VEGA, owner of De La Vega Bodega, 24
NINA ROSARIO, freshman at Stanford, 19
KEVIN ROSARIO, Nina's father, owner of Rosario Car Service, 40s
CAMILA ROSARIO, Nina's mother, co-owner of Rosario's, 40s
BENNY, Rosario Car Service employee, 24
VANESSA, works at the salon, 19
SONNY, Usnavi's cousin, 16
ABUELA CLAUDIA, raised Usnavi, though not his blood grandmother, mid-late 60s
DANIELA, owner of Daniela's Salon, 30s
CARLA, works at the salon, 20s
GRAFFITI PETE, an artist, 18
PIRAGUA GUY, who scrapes piraguas from his block of ice, 30s

PLACE

One block of Washington Heights, Manhattan. On one side of the street is Rosario Car Service with a dispatch booth. Usnavi and Claudia's front stoop is next door. Across the street is De La Vega Bodega and Daniela's Unisex Salon.

Apartment windows and fire escapes tangle into the landscape. A blurry view of the bridge in the background.

TIME

July 3rd through 5th.

MUSICAL NUMBERS

Act 1

Scene 1: Washington Heights—Sunrise
    "In The Heights" — Usnavi and Company

Scene 2: On the Street
    "Breathe" — Nina and Company

Scene 3: Rosario Car Service
    "Benny's Dispatch" — Benny and Nina

Scene 4: The Street
    "It Won't Be Long Now" — Vanessa, Usnavi, and Sonny

Scene 5: The Dispatch Booth
    "Inútil" — Kevin

Scene 6: The Salon
    "No Me Diga" — Daniela, Carla, Vanessa, and Nina

Scene 7: Inside the Bodega; the Street
    "96,000" — Usnavi, Benny, Sonny, Vanessa, Daniela, Carla, and Company

Scene 8: The Street
    "Paciencia y Fe" — Abuela Claudia and Company

Scene 9: Abuela Claudia's Stoop—Early Evening
    "When You're Home" — Nina, Benny, and Company

Scene 10: The Street—Dusk
    "Piragua" — Piragua Guy

Scene 11: The Rosario Household

Scene 12: The Club
    "The Club" — Company
    "Blackout" — Company

Act 2

IN THE HEIGHTS

ACT 1
SCENE 1

(*Sunrise. A radio switches through different stations.*)

RADIO VOICE
Yo, pull out them kiddie pools and call me up with your sizzling summer scandal. Tomorrow's the Fourth of July but we're kicking off the celebration tonight with fireworks at the marina! It's going to be a scorcher!

(*A beat comes in. In the shadows,* GRAFFITI PETE *is revealed painting various walls in the neighborhood. Enter* USNAVI *from his stoop.*)

USNAVI
Yo, that's my wall!

GRAFFITI PETE
Pshh . . .

(GRAFFITI PETE *runs away.* USNAVI *turns to us.*)

"In The Heights"

USNAVI
LIGHTS UP ON WASHINGTON HEIGHTS, UP AT THE BREAK OF DAY.
I WAKE UP AND I GOT THIS LITTLE PUNK I GOTTA CHASE AWAY.
POP THE GRATE AT THE CRACK OF DAWN, SING
WHILE I WIPE DOWN THE AWNING. HEY, Y'ALL, GOOD MORNING.

(USNAVI *opens the bodega.*)

PIRAGUA GUY

(*Scraping from his ice block.*) Ice-cold piragua! Parcha. China. Cherry. Strawberry. Just for today, I got mamey!

USNAVI

Yo, piragüero, como estas?

PIRAGUA GUY

Como siempre, Señor Usnavi.

USNAVI

I AM USNAVI AND YOU PROB'LY NEVER HEARD MY NAME.
REPORTS OF MY FAME ARE GREATLY EXAGGERATED,
EXACERBATED BY THE FACT
THAT MY SYNTAX
IS HIGHLY COMPLICATED 'CUZ I IMMIGRATED FROM THE SINGLE
GREATEST LITTLE PLACE IN THE CARIBBEAN,
DOMINICAN REPUBLIC.
I LOVE IT.
JESUS, I'M JEALOUS OF IT.
BUT BEYOND THAT,
EVER SINCE MY FOLKS PASSED ON,
I HAVEN'T GONE BACK.
GODDAMN, I GOTTA GET ON THAT.

(*He sniffs the milk carton.*) Fo!

THE MILK HAS GONE BAD, HOLD UP JUST A SECOND.
WHY IS EVERYTHING IN THIS FRIDGE WARM AND TEPID?
I BETTER STEP IT UP AND FIGHT THE HEAT.
'CUZ I'M NOT MAKIN' ANY PROFIT
IF THE COFFEE ISN'T LIGHT AND SWEET!

(ABUELA CLAUDIA *enters.*)

IN THE HEIGHTS

ABUELA CLAUDIA

Ooo-oo!

USNAVI

Abuela, do we have milk at home?

ABUELA CLAUDIA

No, que pasó?

USNAVI

It's my fridge. I got café but no "con leche."

ABUELA CLAUDIA

Try my mother's old recipe: one can of condensed milk.

USNAVI

Nice. Your lottery tickets.

ABUELA CLAUDIA

(*She kisses the tickets and holds them up to the sky.*) Paciencia y fe . . .

(*She exits.*)

USNAVI

THAT WAS ABUELA, SHE'S NOT REALLY MY "ABUELA,"
BUT SHE PRACTICALLY RAISED ME, THIS CORNER IS HER ESCUELA!
YOU'RE PROB'LY THINKIN', "I'M UP SHIT'S CREEK!
I NEVER BEEN NORTH OF NINETY-SIXTH STREET."
WELL, YOU MUST TAKE THE A TRAIN
EVEN FARTHER THAN HARLEM TO NORTHERN MANHATTAN AND
MAINTAIN.
GET OFF AT ONE EIGHTY-FIRST, AND TAKE THE ESCALATOR.
I HOPE YOU'RE WRITING THIS DOWN, I'M GONNA TEST YA LATER.
I'M GETTING TESTED, TIMES ARE TOUGH ON THIS BODEGA.
TWO MONTHS AGO SOMEBODY BOUGHT ORTEGA'S
(*Points to the salon.*) OUR NEIGHBORS STARTED PACKIN' UP AND PICKIN' UP
AND EVER SINCE THE RENTS WENT UP

IT'S GOTTEN MAD EXPENSIVE
BUT WE LIVE WITH JUST ENOUGH—

ALL (except NINA)

IN THE HEIGHTS

PIRAGUA GUY/CARLA/DANIELA/OTHERS

I FLIP THE LIGHTS AND START MY DAY

ALL

THERE ARE FIGHTS

CARLA/DANIELA/WOMEN

AND ENDLESS DEBTS

KEVIN/BENNY/PIRAGUA GUY/MEN

AND BILLS TO PAY

ALL

IN THE HEIGHTS

BENNY/KEVIN/PIRAGUA GUY/OTHERS

I CAN'T SURVIVE WITHOUT CAFÉ

USNAVI

I SERVE CAFÉ

ALL

'CUZ TONIGHT SEEMS LIKE A MILLION YEARS AWAY!
EN WASHINGTON—

USNAVI

NEXT UP TO BAT, THE ROSARIOS.
THEY RUN THE CAB COMPANY, THEY STRUGGLE IN THE BARRIO.
SEE, THEIR DAUGHTER NINA'S OFF AT COLLEGE, TUITION IS MAD STEEP.
SO THEY CAN'T SLEEP. EVERYTHING THEY GET IS MAD CHEAP!

(KEVIN *and* CAMILA *enter.*)

KEVIN
GOOD MORNING, USNAVI!

USNAVI
PAN CALIENTE, CAFÉ CON LECHE!

KEVIN
PUT TWENTY DOLLARS ON TODAY'S LOTTERY.

CAMILA
ONE TICKET, THAT'S IT!

KEVIN
HEY! A MAN'S GOTTA DREAM.

CAMILA
DON'T MIND HIM. HE'S ALL EXCITED
'CUZ NINA FLEW IN AT 3 A.M. LAST NIGHT!

KEVIN
DON'T LOOK AT ME. THIS ONE'S BEEN COOKING ALL WEEK!

CAMILA
USNAVI, COME OVER FOR DINNER.

KEVIN/CAMILA
THERE'S PLENTY TO EAT!

(KEVIN *and* CAMILA *exit.* DANIELA *and* CARLA *enter.*)

DANIELA
SO THEN YESENIA WALKS IN THE ROOM—

CARLA
Aha . . .

DANIELA
SHE SMELLS SEX AND CHEAP PERFUME!

CARLA

Uh-oh . . .

DANIELA

IT SMELLS LIKE ONE OF THOSE TREES THAT YOU HANG FROM THE REAR
VIEW!

CARLA

Ah, no!

DANIELA

IT'S TRUE! SHE SCREAMS, "WHO'S IN THERE WITH YOU, JULIO?"
GRABS A BAT AND KICKS IN THE DOOR!
HE'S IN BED WITH JOSÉ FROM THE LIQUOR STORE!

CARLA/USNAVI

NO ME DIGA!

USNAVI

Daniela and Carla, from the salon.

(DANIELA *and* CARLA *grab the stuff and get ready to go.*)

DANIELA/CARLA

THANKS, USNAVI!

(*They exit.* SONNY *runs in.*)

USNAVI

Sonny, you're late.

SONNY

Chillax, you know you love me.

(*He exits.*)

USNAVI

ME AND MY COUSIN RUNNIN' JUST ANOTHER DIME-A-DOZEN

MOM-AND-POP STOP AND SHOP
AND OH MY GOD, IT'S GOTTEN
TOO DARN HOT LIKE MY MAN COLE PORTER SAID.
PEOPLE COME THROUGH FOR A FEW COLD WATERS AND
A LOTTERY TICKET, JUST A PART OF THE ROUTINE.
EVERYBODY'S GOT A JOB, EVERYBODY'S GOT A DREAM.
THEY GOSSIP, AS I SIP MY COFFEE AND SMIRK,
THE FIRST STOP AS PEOPLE HOP TO WORK.
BUST IT— I'M LIKE—

(*People come through his store.*)

ONE DOLLAR, TWO DOLLARS, ONE FIFTY, ONE SIXTY-NINE,
YOU GOT IT. YOU WANT A BOX OF CONDOMS, WHAT KIND?
THAT'S TWO QUARTERS.
TWO QUARTER WATERS. *THE NEW YORK TIMES*—
YOU NEED A BAG FOR THAT? THE TAX IS ADDED.
ONCE YOU GET SOME PRACTICE AT IT
YOU DO RAPID MATHEMATICS AUTOMATICALLY.
SELLIN' MAXIPADS AND FUZZY DICE FOR TAXICABS AND PRACTICALLY
EVERYBODY'S STRESSED, YES, BUT THEY PRESS THROUGH THE MESS
BOUNCE CHECKS AND WONDER, "WHAT'S NEXT?"

ALL

IN THE HEIGHTS

GROUP 1 (USNAVI/CAMILA/CARLA/OTHERS)

I BUY MY COFFEE AND I GO

GROUP 2 (PIRAGUA GUY/FOUR WOMEN/FOUR MEN)

I BUY MY COFFEE AND—

ALL

SET MY SIGHTS

GROUP 1

ON ONLY WHAT I NEED TO KNOW

GROUP 2

WHAT I NEED TO KNOW

ALL

IN THE HEIGHTS
MONEY IS TIGHT

GROUP 1

BUT EVEN SO

GROUP 2

BUT EVEN SO

ALL

WHEN THE LIGHTS GO DOWN I BLAST MY RADIO!

(BENNY *enters, dressed in a shirt and tie like* KEVIN.)

BENNY

YOU AIN'T GOT NO SKILLS!

USNAVI

BENNY!

BENNY

LEMME GET A—

USNAVI

MILKY WAY.

BENNY

YEAH, LEMME ALSO GET A—

USNAVI

DAILY NEWS—

BENNY

AND A—

USNAVI

POST—

BENNY

AND MOST IMPORTANT, MY—

USNAVI

BOSS'S SECOND COFFEE, ONE CREAM—

BOTH

FIVE SUGARS—

BENNY

I'M THE NUMBER-ONE EARNER—

USNAVI

WHAT!

BENNY

THE FASTEST LEARNER—

USNAVI/SONNY

WHAT!?

BENNY

MY BOSS CAN'T KEEP ME ON THE DAMN BACK BURNER!

USNAVI

YES HE CAN.

BENNY

I'M MAKIN' MOVES, I'M MAKIN' DEALS, BUT GUESS WHAT?

USNAVI

WHAT?

BENNY/SONNY

YOU STILL AIN'T GOT NO SKILLS!

USNAVI

HARDEE-HAR.

BENNY

VANESSA SHOW UP YET?

USNAVI

SHUT UP!

BENNY

HEY, LITTLE HOMIE, DON'T GET SO UPSET.
TELL VANESSA HOW YOU FEEL. BUY THE GIRL A MEAL,
ON THE REAL, OR YOU AIN'T GOT NO SKILLS.

(VANESSA *walks by on the phone.*)

VANESSA

NOOO!
NO NO NOOO!
NO NO NOOO, NO NO NO!
NOOO, NO NO NO!
NO NO NO NO NO NO NO NO NO NO NO NO NO!
MR. JOHNSON, I GOT THE SECURITY DEPOSIT.
IT'S LOCKED IN A BOX IN THE BOTTOM OF MY CLOSET.
IT'S NOT REFLECTED IN MY BANK STATEMENT
BUT I'VE BEEN SAVIN' TO MAKE A DOWN PAYMENT AND PAY RENT.
NO, NO, I WON'T LET YOU DOWN.

BENNY

YO, HERE'S YOUR CHANCE, ASK HER OUT RIGHT NOW!

VANESSA

I'LL SEE YOU LATER, WE CAN LOOK AT THAT LEASE! (*She hangs up.*)

BENNY

DO SOMETHIN', MAKE YOUR MOVE, DON'T FREEZE—

USNAVI

HEY!

(VANESSA *approaches* USNAVI.)

VANESSA

YOU OWE ME A BOTTLE OF COLD CHAMPAGNE.

USNAVI

ARE YOU MOVING?

VANESSA

JUST A LITTLE CREDIT CHECK AND I'M ON THAT DOWNTOWN TRAIN!

USNAVI

WELL, YOUR COFFEE'S ON THE HOUSE.

VANESSA

OKAY!

BENNY

(*Under his breath, to* SONNY.) USNAVI, ASK HER OUT.

SONNY

NO WAY!

VANESSA

I'LL SEE YOU LATER, SO . . .

(VANESSA *waits a moment, before exiting.* USNAVI *misses the moment.*)

BENNY

SMOOTH OPERATOR, AW DAMN, THERE SHE GO!
YO, BRO, TAKE FIVE, TAKE A WALK OUTSIDE!
YOU LOOK EXHAUSTED, LOST, DON'T LET LIFE SLIDE!
THE WHOLE HOOD IS STRUGGLING. TIMES ARE TIGHT,
AND YOU'RE STUCK TO THE CORNER LIKE A STREETLIGHT!

USNAVI

YEAH, I'M A STREETLIGHT,
CHOKING ON THE HEAT.
THE WORLD SPINS AROUND
WHILE I'M FROZEN TO MY SEAT.
THE PEOPLE THAT I KNOW
ALL KEEP ON ROLLING DOWN THE STREET.
BUT EVERY DAY IS DIFFERENT
SO I'M SWITCHIN' UP THE BEAT.
'CUZ MY PARENTS CAME WITH NOTHING.
THEY GOT A LITTLE MORE.
AND SURE, WE'RE POOR, BUT YO,
AT LEAST WE GOT THE STORE.
AND IT'S ALL ABOUT THE LEGACY
THEY LEFT WITH ME, IT'S DESTINY.
AND ONE DAY I'LL BE ON A BEACH
WITH SONNY WRITING CHECKS
TO ME.

ENSEMBLE (DANIELA/CARLA/PIRAGUA GUY/OTHERS)

IN THE HEIGHTS I HANG MY FLAG UP ON DISPLAY.

USNAVI

WE CAME TO WORK AND TO LIVE AND WE GOT A LOT IN COMMON.

ENSEMBLE + CAMILA/VANESSA/SONNY/KEVIN

IT REMINDS ME THAT I CAME FROM MILES AWAY.

USNAVI

D.R., P.R., WE ARE NOT STOPPIN'.

ALL	
IN THE HEIGHTS	**ABUELA CLAUDIA**
OOH,	EVERY DAY, PACIENCIA Y FE.
OOH,	
	USNAVI
OOH.	UNTIL THE DAY WE GO FROM
	POVERTY TO STOCK OPTIONS.

ALL

IN THE HEIGHTS
I'VE GOT TODAY.

USNAVI

AND TODAY'S ALL WE GOT, SO WE CANNOT STOP,
THIS IS OUR BLOCK—

ALL

IN THE HEIGHTS
I HANG MY FLAG UP ON DISPLAY

PIRAGUA GUY

LO LE LO LE LO LAI LAI LO LE!

ALL

IT REMINDS ME THAT I CAME FROM MILES AWAY!

USNAVI/PIRAGUA GUY/MAN/WOMAN

MY FAMILY CAME FROM MILES AWAY—

ENSEMBLE

IN THE HEIGHTS
IT GETS MORE EXPENSIVE EVERY DAY

USNAVI/PIRAGUA GUY/MAN/WOMAN

EVERY DAY

ALL

AND TONIGHT IS SO FAR AWAY—

USNAVI

AS FOR MAÑANA MI PANA YA GOTTA JUST KEEP WATCHIN',

USNAVI	BENNY/GRAFFITI	ALL OTHERS
YOU'LL SEE THE	PETE/THREE MEN	IN THE HEIGHTS
LATE NIGHTS,	LATE NIGHTS,	
YOU'LL TASTE		
BEANS AND RICE,	BEANS AND RICE,	
THE SYRUPS AND		IN THE HEIGHTS
SHAVED ICE,	SHAVED ICE,	
I AIN'T GONNA		
SAY IT TWICE.	SAY IT TWICE.	
		IN THE HEIGHTS

USNAVI		
SO TURN UP THE		**ALL**
STAGE LIGHTS,	AH	
WE'RE TAKIN' A FLIGHT	AH	
TO A COUPLE OF DAYS	AH	
IN THE LIFE OF WHAT IT'S LIKE—		

ALL

EN WASHINGTON HEIGHTS!

SCENE 2

(USNAVI *and* SONNY *are out on the street.* ABUELA CLAUDIA *sits on her stoop.*)

USNAVI

What did I say? Go fix the fridge.

SONNY

Hells no, it was blowing fuses, sparking and shit!

ABUELA CLAUDIA

Usnavi, send him to D.R. for the summer. Let him work on a farm so his Nikes can get real dirt on them!

USNAVI

I ain't wastin' no plane ticket on this kid. I'll be on Playa Rincón with a rum and

14

Coke. Sonny can stay here and sell Twinkies.

SONNY

Sell? I'll give them out free, I'm the Robin Hood of el barrio.

(*He exits.* NINA *enters, looks around the neighborhood.*)

NINA

Hey!

USNAVI

Nina Rosario, what is up?

NINA

Jetlag, I haven't slept all night.

ABUELA CLAUDIA

It's the watermelon of my heart!

NINA

Bendición, Abuela.

ABUELA CLAUDIA

Congratulations, your first year at Stanford University!

NINA

It felt like ten.

ABUELA CLAUDIA

You just missed your parents.

NINA

I'm here to see you guys.

USNAVI

So, did you kick some college ass?

NINA

I got mine handed to me on a silver platter.

ABUELA CLAUDIA

Please, you knew the state capitals when you were in diapers.

USNAVI

You registered half this block to vote!

ABUELA CLAUDIA

The future mayor of Nueva York!

(SONNY *enters.*)

SONNY

I wanna be your campaign manager . . . Yo, miss, recognize this face?

NINA

Look who's a grown man.

SONNY

Check outs the goatee.

USNAVI

That's fridge grease.

SONNY

Why you so jealous of my skills?

USNAVI

Back to work.

(SONNY *exits.*)

(*To* NINA.) Stop by later!

(USNAVI *exits.*)

NINA

Those recipes you sent were my survival kit.

ABUELA CLAUDIA

I had to make sure you remembered the flavor of home. (*Gets up.*) Bueno, come inside, I have your sandwichito ready!

NINA

I'll be there in a second.

ABUELA CLAUDIA

I'll go put the fan on.

(ABUELA CLAUDIA *exits into her apartment.*)

"Breathe"

PIRAGUA GUY

SIGUE ANDANDO EL CAMINO POR TODA SU VIDA. RESPIRA.

NINA	PIRAGUA GUY/SONNY/USNAVI/MAN
BREATHE.	Y SI PIERDAS MIS HUELLAS QUE
	DIOS TE BENDIGA.
	RESPIRA.

NINA

THIS IS MY STREET.
I SMILE AT THE FACES
I'VE KNOWN ALL MY LIFE. THEY REGARD ME WITH PRIDE.
AND EVERYONE'S SWEET.
THEY SAY, "YOU'RE GOING PLACES!"
SO HOW CAN I SAY THAT WHILE I WAS AWAY I HAD SO MUCH TO HIDE?
HEY, GUYS, IT'S ME!
THE BIGGEST DISAPPOINTMENT YOU KNOW.
THE KID COULDN'T HACK IT, SHE'S BACK AND SHE'S WALKIN' REAL SLOW.
WELCOME HOME.
JUST BREATHE . . .

ENSEMBLE (USNAVI/SONNY/DANIELA/OTHERS)

SIGUE ANDANDO EL CAMINO POR TODA SU VIDA.
RESPIRA.

NINA	**ENSEMBLE**
JUST BREATHE—	Y SI PIERDES MIS HUELLAS QUE
	DIOS TE BENDIGA.
	RESPIRA.

NINA

AS THE RADIO PLAYS OLD FORGOTTEN BOLEROS
I THINK OF THE DAYS WHEN THIS CITY WAS MINE.
I REMEMBER THE PRAISE,

NINA	**ENSEMBLE**
"AY, TE ADORO, TE QUIERO."	TE ADORO,
THE NEIGHBORHOOD WAVED AND	
SAID, "NINA, BE BRAVE AND	TE QUIERO,
YOU'RE GONNA BE FINE."	RESPIRA!
AND MAYBE IT'S ME, BUT IT ALL	
SEEMS LIKE LIFETIMES AGO.	RESPIRA!

NINA

SO WHAT DO I SAY TO THESE FACES THAT I USED TO KNOW?
"HEY, I'M HOME"?

WOMAN

MIRA, NINA—

NINA

HEY.

CARLA/DANIELA/PIRAGUA GUY/OTHERS

NO ME PREOCUPO POR ELLA.

NINA

THEY'RE NOT WORRIED ABOUT ME.

CARLA/DANIELA/PIRAGUA GUY/OTHERS

MIRA, ALLI ESTA NUESTRA ESTRELLA—

NINA	ENSEMBLE + SONNY/USNAVI/ OTHERS
THEY ARE ALL COUNTING ON ME TO SUCCEED.	ELLA SI DA LA TALLA . . .
I AM THE ONE WHO MADE IT OUT!	AH! AH, AAH—
THE ONE WHO ALWAYS MADE THE GRADE.	
BUT MAYBE I SHOULD HAVE JUST STAYED HOME . . .	MIRA, NINA!

NINA

WHEN I WAS A CHILD I STAYED WIDE AWAKE, CLIMBED TO THE HIGHEST PLACE, ON EVERY FIRE ESCAPE, RESTLESS TO CLIMB—

ENSEMBLE

RESPIRA—

NINA

JUST ME AND THE GWB. ASKING, "GEE, NINA, WHAT'LL YOU BE?"

NINA	ENSEMBLE
I GOT EVERY SCHOLARSHIP, SAVED EVERY DOLLAR,	
THE FIRST TO GO TO COLLEGE, HOW DO I TELL THEM WHY	RESPIRA—
I'M COMING BACK HOME? WITH MY EYES ON THE HORIZON.	AHH—

STRAIGHTEN THE SPINE.
SMILE FOR THE NEIGHBORS.
EVERYTHING'S FINE.
EVERYTHING'S COOL.
THE STANDARD REPLY,
"LOTS OF TESTS, LOTS OF PAPERS."

SMILE, WAVE GOODBYE,
AND PRAY TO THE SKY, OH GOD,
AND WHAT WILL MY PARENTS SAY?

                    ENSEMBLE (CARLA/DANIELA/USNAVI/OTHERS)
NINA—

                              NINA
CAN I GO IN THERE AND SAY,

                              ENSEMBLE
NINA—

                              NINA
"I KNOW THAT I'M LETTING YOU DOWN . . ."

    (ABUELA CLAUDIA *appears at the stoop again.*)

                         ABUELA CLAUDIA
NINA—

                              NINA
JUST BREATHE . . .

    (*She exits into* ABUELA CLAUDIA*'s apartment.*)

SCENE 3

    (*Rosario Car Service.* CAMILA *is going through bills.*)

                              KEVIN
(*Into the radio.*) Ciento noventa y dos, en la esquina, al frente del McDonald's.
(*Beat.*) Atención, I know it's hot but I don't want to see any drivers without a
tie, this is Rosario's. (*Cozies up to* CAMILA.) How can you be stressed when our
muñeca's home?

CAMILA

The mechanic called, he won't touch another engine till we pay for last month.

KEVIN

Then I'll get a little engine grease on my hands.

CAMILA

Why, so you can hurt your back again?

KEVIN

You used to think I was sexy when I fixed cars.

CAMILA

Before all that mileage . . . (*Looking at a letter.*) Mira, Uptown Investment Group . . .

KEVIN

Another developer. It's not an offer, it's an insult.

CAMILA

Regency Bank. (*Opens a letter.*) We're behind on all these payments. We need an emergency loan.

KEVIN

We'll go see the bank manager Monday.

CAMILA

This can't wait, Papi.

KEVIN

The dispatcher called out.

BENNY

Hey, boss, I'll cover the radio.

KEVIN

You don't speak Spanish.

BENNY

Five years with these drivers?

KEVIN

You're not Latino.

CAMILA

How much English did you speak when you started here? Benny is honorary Latino.

(KEVIN *hands* BENNY *the radio.*)

BENNY

Ahem, there's a new voice riding the heat wave today—

KEVIN

Just get them from point A to point B.

BENNY

I got your back.

(CAMILA *and* KEVIN *exit.*)

"Benny's Dispatch"

BENNY

CHECK ONE, TWO, THREE. CHECK ONE, TWO, THREE
THIS IS BENNY ON THE DISPATCH. YO.
ATENCIÓN, YO, ATTENTION,
IT'S BENNY, AND I'D LIKE TO MENTION
I'M ON THE MICROPHONE THIS MORNIN'
HONK YA HORN IF YOU WANT IT.

(*Car horns blast.* NINA *exits* CLAUDIA*'s apartment, enters the dispatch.*)

OKAY, WE GOT TRAFFIC ON THE WEST SIDE.
GET OFF AT SEVENTY-NINTH, AND TAKE THE LEFT SIDE

OF RIVERSIDE DRIVE, AND YA MIGHT SLIDE.
WEST END'S YA BEST FRIEND IF YOU CATCH THE LIGHTS!
AND DON'T TAKE THE DEEGAN.
MANNY RAMIREZ IS IN TOWN THIS WEEKEND.
SORRY, DOMINICANS, TAKE ROUTE EIGHTY-SEVEN, YOU AIN'T GETTING
BACK IN AGAIN.
HOLD UP A MINUTE—

(*He puts down the radio.*)

NINA

BENNY, HEY—

BENNY

NINA, YOU'RE HOME TODAY!

NINA

ANY SIGN—

BENNY

OF YOUR FOLKS, THEY'RE ON THEIR WAY!

NINA

ANYWAY—

BENNY

IT'S GOOD TO SEE YOUR FACE—

NINA

ANYTIME—

BENNY

HOLD UP A MINUTE, WAIT!
YOU USED TO RUN THIS DISPATCH, RIGHT?

NINA

ONCE OR TWICE—

BENNY

WELL, CHECK THE TECHNIQUE! YO!
(*Into the dispatch.*) THERE'S A TRAFFIC ACCIDENT I HAVE TO MENTION
AT THE INTERSECTION OF TENTH AVE AND THE JACOB JAVITS
CONVENTION CENTER.
AND CHECK IT, DON'T GET STUCK IN THE RUBBER-NECKIN'
ON A HUNDRED NINETY-SECOND,
THERE'S A DOUBLE-DECKER BUS WRECK!
AND LISTEN UP, WE GOT A SPECIAL GUEST!

BENNY	NINA
LIVE AND DIRECT FROM A YEAR OUT WEST!	BENNY . . .
WELCOME HER BACK, SHE LOOKS MAD STRESSED! NINA ROSARIO, THE BARRIO'S BEST! HONK YOUR HORNS . . .	BENNY . . .

(*We hear a series of syncopated horn blasts, as* BENNY *continues to sing.*)

SHE'S SMILING . . . SAY HELLO!

(NINA *steps to the microphone.*)

NINA

HELLO . . .

(*We hear the cacophony of the most beautiful horn chart ever written.*)

GOOD MORNING!

(NINA *catches herself having fun, abruptly stops.*)

I BETTER FIND MY FOLKS.
THANKS FOR THE WELCOME WAGON.

IN THE HEIGHTS

BENNY

ANYTIME. ANYTIME, NINA.

(NINA *heads for the door.* BENNY *stops her.*)

WAIT HERE WITH ME.
IT'S GETTING HOT OUTSIDE. TURN UP THE A.C.
STAY HERE WITH ME.

(*She sits beside him. Big button!*)

"Everything Is Melting"

DANIELA/CARLA/SONNY/OTHERS

WHOAA!
OH!
WHOAA!
OH!

SCENE 4

(ABUELA CLAUDIA *is on her stoop, feeding pigeons.* USNAVI *enters from the bodega.*)

USNAVI

Oye, you missed another doctor's appointment.

ABUELA CLAUDIA

Mijo, would you take medical advice from a man named Dr. Gross?

USNAVI

As long as you're taking your medicine.

(ABUELA CLAUDIA *doesn't respond.*)

Abuela . . . No puedes olvidar—

ABUELA CLAUDIA

It makes my heart work better, but in return it gives me headaches. Imagínate, with what those pills cost, I could get myself a good facelift. (*Demonstrating nips and tucks on her face.*) Sácalo de aquí, mételo pacá. Sácalo de aquí, mételo pacá. Pacá, pacá . . .

(SONNY *comes out of the bodega with a soda in hand.*)

SONNY

Who hooked it up? Ice-cold country-club cola champagne! Ahhhhhh.

USNAVI

Put that on your tab. You owe me five thousand, three hundred—

ABUELA CLAUDIA

Usnavi, I think he's trying to tell you, he fixed the Frigidaire.

SONNY

So let's talk about that raise. Free sodas or I walk.

USNAVI

Half price. Diet. Cola champagne. That's my final offer.

(*He exits.*)

SONNY

Ain't no Dominicans be drinking no diet soda!

VANESSA

(*From across the street.*) Be thankful, at least someone around here is getting a raise!

SONNY

I'm starting a union. Underage cousins of bodega workers unite! (*Exits into the bodega.*)

(*Lights shift to the salon.* VANESSA *is outside on her phone.* DANIELA *comes out of the salon.*)

DANIELA

Excuse me, this isn't social hours.

VANESSA

Sorry, it's Con Edison. I gave my mom half my check to pay the bills . . .

DANIELA

Y que pasó? She drank it away? Vanessa, when are you going to get out of that toxic environment?

VANESSA

(*Into the phone.*) Hi, ma'am? I get my check on Monday, I can pay then. Yes, I'll hold. (*To* DANIELA.) Daniela, I know I still owe you from last time . . .

DANIELA

Carla, what's my rule?

CARLA

(*To* VANESSA.) She'll do anything for you but she won't support your mother's malfunction . . .

DANIELA

(*Correcting her.*) Dysfunction.

VANESSA

My lights are going to be out all week.

CARLA

What would Jesus do?

DANIELA

Do I look like Jesus to you?

VANESSA

(*Into the phone.*) I'm still here. Don't transfer me! Hello? Hello?

DANIELA

(*Takes the phone.*) Comay, it's time to clear out that negative energy! So take five and get me some packing tape.

VANESSA

Anything else? While I'm at it?

DANIELA

A Pepsi. (*Exiting, to* CARLA.) Tough love, chacha.

(DANIELA *and* CARLA *exit into the salon.*)

"It Won't Be Long Now"

VANESSA

THE ELEVATED TRAIN BY MY WINDOW DOESN'T FAZE ME ANYMORE.
THE RATTLING SCREAMS DON'T DISRUPT MY DREAMS.
IT'S A LULLABY, IN ITS WAY.
THE ELEVATED TRAIN DRIVES EVERYONE INSANE, BUT I DON'T MIND, OH NO.
WHEN I BRING BACK BOYS, THEY CAN'T TOLERATE THE NOISE
AND THAT'S OKAY, 'CUZ I NEVER LET THEM STAY.
AND ONE DAY, I'M HOPPIN' ON THAT ELEVATED TRAIN AND I'M RIDING AWAY!
IT WON'T BE LONG NOW!

(*Men whistle at* VANESSA *on the sidewalk.*)

THE BOYS AROUND THE WAY HOLLER AT ME WHEN I'M WALKING DOWN THE STREET.
THEIR MACHISMO PRIDE DOESN'T BREAK MY STRIDE—
IT'S A COMPLIMENT, SO THEY SAY.
THE BOYS AROUND THE WAY HOLLER AT ME EVERY DAY, BUT I DON'T MIND, OH NO.
IF I'M IN THE MOOD, IT WILL NOT BE WITH SOME DUDE
WHO IS WHISTLING 'CUZ HE HAS NOTHING TO SAY.
OR WHO'S HONKING AT ME FROM HIS CHEVROLET.
AND ONE DAY . . . I'M HOPPIN' IN A LIMOUSINE AND I'M DRIVING AWAY!
IT WON'T BE LONG NOW!

(VANESSA *approaches* USNAVI *outside the bodega.*)

Ay, Usnavi, help! SOS!

USNAVI

GOOD MORNING, VANESSA!
IF IT ISN'T THE LOVELIEST GIRL IN THE PLACE.

(*She wipes his cheek.*)

VANESSA

YOU GOT SOME SCHMUTZ ON YOUR FACE.

USNAVI

Another late night, eh? Whoever you were with, he's got nothing on these biceps.
I bench-press six gallons of milk and two cases of Goya beans.

VANESSA

It was my mom. They shut our power off. Again.

USNAVI

Coffee. Whole milk. Very sweet. Little bit of cinnamon.

VANESSA

Mm. Just like my abuela used to do.

USNAVI

That's what all the ladies say. I remind them of their grandma.

SONNY

GOOD MORNING!

SONNY/USNAVI

GOOD MORNING!

(VANESSA *kisses* SONNY *on the cheek. She grabs* SONNY *to dance.*)

USNAVI

VANESSA . . .

SONNY

VANESSA . . .

USNAVI/SONNY

VANESSA . . .

DANIELA

(*Screaming from the salon.*) VANESSSSSAAAAAA! I'm thirsty, coño!

VANESSA

Can I get a Pepsi and some packing tape?

SONNY

Uh, my cousin over there with his tongue hanging out, has been meaning to ask you . . .

VANESSA

Yes?

SONNY

What a lady such as yourself might be doing tonight?

VANESSA

Does your cousin dance?

SONNY

Like a drunk Chita Rivera.

VANESSA

Okay . . . After Nina's dinner, we can hit a few clubs and check out the fireworks . . .

(USNAVI *awkwardly hands her a bag. She exits.*)

USNAVI

OH SNAP! WHO'S THAT? DON'T TOUCH ME, I'M TOO HOT! YES!
QUE PASÓ? HERE I GO! SO DOPE! Y TU LO SABES!
NO PARE—

SONNY/USNAVI

SIGUE SIGUE!

USNAVI

DID YOU SEE ME—

SONNY/USNAVI

FREAKY FREAK IT!

USNAVI

WHAT A WAY TO BEGIN THE WEEKEND! SONNY, ANYTHING YOU WANT IS
FREE, MAN!
AND MY DEARLY BELOVED DOMINICAN REPUBLIC
I HAVEN'T FORGOTTEN

SONNY/USNAVI

YOU!

USNAVI

GONNA SEE THIS HONEY, MAKE A LITTLE MONEY
AND ONE DAY I'LL HOP

SONNY/USNAVI

JET BLUE!

USNAVI

BUT UNTIL THAT FATEFUL DAY, I'M GRATEFUL
I GOT A DESTINATION.
I'M RUNNIN' TO MAKE IT HOME AND HOME'S WHAT VANESSA'S RUNNIN'
AWAY FROM!
I'M RUNNIN' TO MAKE IT HOME AND HOME'S WHAT VANESSA'S RUNNIN'
AWAY FROM . . .

(USNAVI *is at the bodega door,* VANESSA *at the salon door. She sings to him.*)

VANESSA

THE NEIGHBORHOOD SALON IS THE PLACE I'M WORKING FOR THE MOMENT.
AS I CUT THEIR HAIR, LADIES TALK AND SHARE—
EVERY DAY, WHO'S DOING WHO AND WHY.
THE NEIGHBORHOOD SALON DOESN'T PAY ME WHAT I WANNA BE MAKING, BUT I DON'T MIND.
AS I SWEEP THE CURB, I CAN HEAR THOSE TURBO
ENGINES BLAZING A TRAIL THROUGH THE SKY.
I LOOK UP AND THINK ABOUT THE YEARS GONE BY
BUT ONE DAY—I'M WALKIN' TO JFK AND I'M GONNA FLY!
IT WON'T BE LONG NOW!
ANY DAY . . .

(*They exit.*)

SCENE 5

(BENNY *and* NINA *in the dispatch booth.*)

BENNY

(*Into the radio. Shaky Spanish.*) Roger. Cómo? Uh . . . dónde estás? Uno momento. Yo, cabrón, I'm trying to help you!

NINA

Whoa, who taught you Spanish?

BENNY

The drivers, dirty bastards.

NINA

(*Takes the radio.*) Aha, dime. (*Listens.*) He's going to the Cloisters, he's stuck on the Hudson.

BENNY

Exit fourteen, follow signs to Fort Tryon.

NINA

The U-turn off exit fifteen is quicker.

BENNY

It's also illegal.

NINA

(*Into the radio.*) Salida quince, hagas una media vuelta, sigue derecho.

BENNY

You gave him your directions, didn't you?

(KEVIN *enters, watching* BENNY *and* NINA *flirt.*)

KEVIN

Eyes on the dispatch, por favor.

BENNY

(*Back to work.*) Yes, sir.

KEVIN

(*Hugs* NINA.) You look more beautiful and even smarter!

NINA

It must be the bags under my eyes.

(CAMILA *enters.*)

CAMILA

Nena de mamá! Mija tan preciosa! Turn around, let me see my flaquita!

NINA

Mom.

CAMILA

Excuse me, you think you're all grown up?

NINA

I was hoping we could grab a few coffees and go home for a minute.

KEVIN

No, we're celebrating! Caridad is still serving breakfast.

NINA

I ate at Abuela Claudia's.

CAMILA

So? I get to fatten you up, too!

KEVIN

We have to go by Daniela's. Everyone wants to see you.

NINA

You guys! (*Beat.*) Okay. I planned this whole speech on the plane . . .

KEVIN

Benny, give us a minute.

BENNY

(*To* NINA.) If there's anything I can do . . .

KEVIN

Go.

(BENNY *exits.*)

CAMILA

Mija.

NINA

I lost my scholarship.

CAMILA

Did you get in some kind of trouble?

NINA

No.

CAMILA

It's okay. Just tell us what happened.

NINA

My grades were below the cutoff, so they put me on probation. After midterms they called me into the dean's office and he was like, "We have to pull your scholarship."

CAMILA

But you were studying nonstop!

NINA

No, I was working to pay for books I didn't have time to read. Look, I ended up taking a leave of absence.

CAMILA

Does leave of absence mean drop out? Nina, look at me.

NINA

I guess you could say I left school.

KEVIN

What?

CAMILA

Oh my God, when?

NINA

I didn't know what to do—

CAMILA

When?

ACT 1

35

NINA

March.

CAMILA

Four months ago!? What were you doing since then?

NINA

Figuring out how to tell you. Staying on my friend's couch.

CAMILA

Like a beggar? You lied to me! Every time I called you!

NINA

I couldn't work two jobs and study for finals and finish my term papers.

KEVIN

Two jobs? You said it was going to be one.

NINA

It's expensive. The scholarship only covered part of it.

KEVIN

Then you pick up the phone and say, "Papi, I need some money."

NINA

You laid off half your drivers this year.

KEVIN

I would have found a way!

NINA

You don't know what college is like!

KEVIN

Well then, educate me, por favor!

(*Pause.*)

CAMILA

I'm going to get started on dinner.

NINA

Cancel tonight.

CAMILA

You be home in an hour!

(*She exits.*)

KEVIN

Why didn't you just ask me?

NINA

What could you have done?

(*She exits.*)

"Inútil"

KEVIN

THIS ISN'T HAPPENING.
INÚTIL. USELESS.
JUST LIKE MY FATHER WAS BEFORE ME.
INÚTIL. USELESS.
AND EVERY DAY,
HE CUT THE CANE,
HE CAME HOME LATE AND PRAYED FOR RAIN. PRAYED FOR RAIN.

AND ON THE DAYS
WHEN NOTHING CAME
MY FATHER'S FACE WAS LINED WITH SHAME.
HE'D SIT ME DOWN BESIDE HIM AND HE'D SAY,
"MY FATHER WAS A FARMER.
HIS FATHER WAS A FARMER,
AND YOU WILL BE A FARMER."

BUT I TOLD HIM, "PAPI, I'M SORRY, I'M GOING FARTHER.
I'M GETTING ON A PLANE.
AND I AM GONNA CHANGE THE WORLD SOMEDAY."
AND HE SLAPPED MY FACE.
HE STOOD THERE, STARING AT ME, USELESS.
TODAY MY DAUGHTER'S HOME AND I AM USELESS.

AND AS A BABY SHE AMAZED ME WITH
THE THINGS SHE LEARNED EACH DAY.
SHE USED TO STAY ON THE FIRE ESCAPE
WHILE ALL THE OTHER KIDS WOULD PLAY.
AND I WOULD STAND BESIDE HER AND I'D SAY:

"I'M PROUD TO BE YOUR FATHER,
'CUZ YOU WORK SO MUCH HARDER
AND YOU ARE SO MUCH SMARTER
THAN I WAS AT YOUR AGE."
AND I ALWAYS KNEW THAT SHE WOULD FLY AWAY.
THAT SHE WAS GONNA CHANGE THE WORLD SOMEDAY.

I WILL NOT BE THE REASON
THAT MY FAMILY CAN'T SUCCEED.
I WILL DO WHAT IT TAKES.
THEY'LL HAVE EVERYTHING THEY NEED
OR ALL MY WORK, ALL MY LIFE
EVERYTHING I'VE SACRIFICED WILL HAVE BEEN USELESS.

SCENE 6

(*The salon.* DANIELA, CARLA, *and* VANESSA *are packing.*)

DANIELA

You know me, I don't like to talk about nobody, pero . . . oye esto!

CARLA

Dani, don't! My pastor told me gossip is a sin.

DANIELA

Jesus, perdóname. Gladys went behind my back for a ten-dollar hairdo and guess what she found in her extensions? Una cucaracha. One of the big ones, with wings.

(NINA *enters.*)

NINA

Hey, ladies . . .

DANIELA

Entre, mija!

CARLA

Mira quien es!

VANESSA

Hells yeah, she's back!

NINA

(*To* VANESSA.) I called you all morning.

VANESSA

Guess who confiscated my phone? Next fall, put me in your suitcase and take me with you.

NINA

(*To* DANIELA.) Mind if I steal Vanessa for a minute?

DANIELA

And what are we, chopped chuletas?

CARLA

Pobrecita, you need a makeover.

NINA

I have to go help my mom . . . I'll see you at dinner?

DANIELA

I'll be packing. Tomorrow we close that door forever!

NINA

Oh no. (*Sits.*) Alright, ten minutes.

DANIELA

Can you believe the salon's moving to the Bronx?

VANESSA

Gettin' out the barrio, and headin' to the hood.

DANIELA

(*To* NINA.) They keep raising the rent, what can I do?

NINA

Man, now who's going to mess up my highlights?

DANIELA

Ungrateful! I mess up your highlights at a discount price. And if you come visit in the Bronx, free eyebrow waxing!

NINA

You're the only person who touches these brows.

DANIELA

So I see. Tweezers!

(VANESSA *hands* DANIELA *tweezers.*)

CARLA

What happened to these curls? You need some hair gel, Mami.

NINA

Oh God, do not make my hair all crunchy!

DANIELA

You have to accept hair gel into your life!

"No Me Diga"

DANIELA

GORGEOUS!

CARLA

LINDA!

CARLA/DANIELA

TELL ME SOMETHING I DON'T KNOW!

VANESSA

VIEJA!

DANIELA

SUCIA!

CARLA

CABRONA!

CARLA/VANESSA/DANIELA

TELL ME SOMETHING I DON'T KNOW!

CARLA

A LITTLE OFF THE TOP—

DANIELA

A LITTLE ON THE SIDE—

NINA

A LITTLE BIT OF NEWS YOU'VE HEARD AROUND THE BARRIO!

ALL

TELL ME SOMETHING I DON'T KNOW!

DANIELA

BUENO.
YOU DIDN'T HEAR THIS FROM ME!

BUT SOME LITTLE BIRDIE TOLD ME
USNAVI HAD SEX WITH YOLANDA!

NINA/CARLA

NO ME DIGA!

VANESSA

AY, NO! HE'D NEVER GO OUT WITH A SKANK LIKE THAT!
PLEASE TELL ME YOU'RE JOKING!

DANIELA

OKAY!
JUST WANTED TO SEE WHAT YOU'D SAY!

ALL

WOOOOOOOOO!
TELL ME SOMETHING I DON'T KNOW!

CARLA/NINA/DANIELA

(*At* VANESSA.) MMM-HMM-MMM . . .

VANESSA

What? I don't care!

ALL

AY BENDITO!

DANIELA

SO, NINA, I HEAR YOU BEEN TALKING TO BENNY.

NINA

AND WHAT DO YOU HEAR?

DANIELA

I HEAR PLENTY.
THEY SAY HE'S GOT QUITE A BIG . . . TAXI!

CARLA/VANESSA

NO ME DIGA!

NINA

OKAY! I DON'T WANNA KNOW WHERE YOU HEARD ALL THAT!

CARLA

I DON'T THINK I KNOW WHAT YOU MEAN . . .

DANIELA

CARLA! HE'S PACKING A STRETCH LIMOUSINE!

(CARLA *gets it. They all laugh.*)

VANESSA/DANIELA

TELL ME SOMETHING I DON'T KNOW!

CARLA

LONG AS HE KEEPS IT CLEAN!

NINA/VANESSA/DANIELA

AY DIOS MIO . . .

(*The women hoot and holler.*)

DANIELA

NINA, SERIOUSLY, WE KNEW YOU'D BE THE ONE TO MAKE IT OUT!

VANESSA

I'LL BET YOU IMPRESSED THEM ALL OUT WEST. YOU WERE ALWAYS THE BEST, NO DOUBT!

CARLA

WE WANT FRONT-ROW SEATS TO YOUR GRADUATION—

DANIELA

THEY'LL CALL YOUR NAME—

DANIELA/CARLA/VANESSA

AND WE'LL SCREAM AND SHOUT!

(*They cheer for* NINA. *The music stops.*)

NINA

You guys, I dropped out.

DANIELA/CARLA/VANESSA

No me diga?!

NINA

I should go.

(*She exits.*)

DANIELA

That's a shitty piece of news.

CARLA

That girl never quit anything.

DANIELA

Muchacha never got a B!

VANESSA

She got a C in gym once. I had to talk her off the fire escape.

DANIELA

Maybe the pressure cooker couldn't take it and pah, the lid flew off!

VANESSA

But why? What the hell happened?

DANIELA

I DON'T KNOW . . .

I DON'T KNOW.

DANIELA

I DON'T KNOW!

CARLA/VANESSA

TELL ME SOMETHING I DON'T KNOW!

ALL

QUÉ SE YO?

SCENE 7

(*Inside the bodega.* USNAVI *is checking lottery numbers.* BENNY *is there fanning himself.*)

BENNY

Does my tie look straight?

USNAVI

Benny, you look the same as every day. Quit trying to impress Nina.

SONNY

(*Sniffs.*) Whoo, you need to impress some Old Spice under those arms.

BENNY

Shut up. My boss put me on dispatch, I need to look professional.

SONNY

"My boss, my boss." You're paving the road to someone else's dreams. Man, strike out on your own.

BENNY

I'm learning on someone else's dime. The day I open Benny's Car Service, I'll know my trade inside and out.

USNAVI

Either one of you Rockefellers wanna take this business off my hands?

SONNY	**BENNY**
Heck no.	Naw, I'm cool.

USNAVI

Yeah, I thought so.

(GRAFFITI PETE *enters, displaying a hand-airbrushed T-shirt.*)

GRAFFITI PETE

What up? Buy my T-shirt.

USNAVI

That's your sales pitch? Get the hell out of here.

GRAFFITI PETE

Today's special, two for twenty.

USNAVI

How about I give you nothing and you scrub your initials off my awning?

SONNY

(*Hands* PETE *a slushie.*) Sonny's secret recipe.

USNAVI

That's a dollar twenty-five.

GRAFFITI PETE

Let's trade. I got some Roman candles, bottle rockets. Third of July, party starts tonight!

USNAVI

Contraband. Vandalism. You got three seconds before I call the cops. 9. 1.

(GRAFFITI PETE *exits.*)

SONNY

Usnavi, double-check this. (*Hands* USNAVI *the paper.*)

USNAVI

Take Five Lotto. Hold up, we sold a winner yesterday?

BENNY

Somebody won?

SONNY

Yo, I want a cut of your cut!

USNAVI

I don't get a cut. Yup, these numbers match!

BENNY

What's the payout? Don't tell me no five hundred dollars.

"96,000"

USNAVI

NINETY-SIX THOUSAND.

SONNY/BENNY

DAMN.

USNAVI

NINETY-SIX THOUSAND.

(GRAFFITI PETE *pokes his head back in, still with the slushie.*)

SONNY

DOLLARS? HOLLER.

USNAVI

NINETY-SIX THOUSAND.

GRAFFITI PETE

THAT'S A LOT OF SPRAY CANS . . .

USNAVI

NINETY-SIX THOUSAND.

BENNY

YO.
IF I WON THE LOTTO TOMORROW
WELL, I KNOW I WOULDN'T BOTHER GOIN' ON NO
SPENDIN' SPREE.
I'D PICK A BUSINESS SCHOOL AND PAY THE ENTRANCE FEE!
THEN MAYBE IF YOU'RE LUCKY, YOU'LL STAY FRIENDS WITH ME!
I'LL BE A BUSINESSMAN, RICHER THAN NINA'S DADDY!
DONALD TRUMP AND I ON THE LINKS, AND HE'S MY CADDY!
MY MONEY'S MAKIN' MONEY, I'M GOIN' FROM PO' TO MO' DOUGH!
KEEP THE BLING, I WANT THE BRASS RING, LIKE FRODO!

USNAVI

OH, NO! HERE GOES MR. BRAGGADOCIO!
NEXT THING YOU KNOW, HE'S LYING LIKE PINOCCHIO—

BENNY

WELL, IF YOU'RE SCARED OF THE BULL, STAY OUT THE RODEO!

GRAFFITI PETE

YO, I GOT MORE HOS THAN A PHONE BOOK IN TOKYO!

USNAVI

OOH, YOU BETTER STOP RAPPIN'. YOU'RE NOT READY.
IT'S GONNA GET HOT AND HEAVY, AND YOU'RE ALREADY SWEATY—

GRAFFITI PETE

Y-Y-YO-YO—

USNAVI

I'M SORRY, WAS THAT AN ANSWER?
SHUT UP, GO HOME AND PULL YA DAMN PANTS UP!

AS FOR YOU, MR. FRODO OF THE SHIRE—
NINETY-SIX G'S AIN'T ENOUGH TO RETIRE.

BENNY

I'LL HAVE ENOUGH TO KNOCK YOUR ASS OFF ITS AXIS!

USNAVI

YOU'LL HAVE A KNAPSACK FULL OF JACK AFTER TAXES!

(SONNY *runs to* ABUELA CLAUDIA.)

SONNY

NINETY-SIX THOUSAND!

ABUELA CLAUDIA

(*Crosses herself.*) Ay alabanza!

(ABUELA CLAUDIA *disappears into her apartment.* SONNY *runs to the salon.*)

SONNY

NINETY-SIX THOUSAND!

DANIELA

No me diga!

SONNY

NINETY-SIX THOUSAND!

VANESSA

I never win shit!

SONNY

NINETY-SIX THOUSAND!

(CARLA *and* DANIELA *come out to the street.*)

BENNY

FOR REAL, THOUGH. IMAGINE HOW IT WOULD FEEL GOIN' REAL SLOW
DOWN THE HIGHWAY OF LIFE WITH NO REGRETS
AND NO BREAKIN' YOUR NECK FOR RESPECT OR A PAYCHECK.
FOR REAL, THOUGH. I'LL TAKE A BREAK FROM THE WHEEL AND WE'LL
THROW
THE BIGGEST BLOCK PARTY, EVERYBODY HERE!
A WEEKEND WHEN WE CAN BREATHE, TAKE IT EASY—

MAN/TWO WOMEN

YO! MA, IT'S ME! CHECK MY TICKETS!

CARLA

CHECK ONE, TWO, THREE!
WHAT WOULD YOU DO WITH NINETY-SIX G'S—

DANIELA

WHO, ME?

CARLA

I MEAN, IF IT'S JUST BETWEEN YOU AND ME—

DANIELA

ESA PREGUNTA ES TRICKY!

CARLA

I KNOW.

DANIELA

WITH NINETY-SIX G'S
I'D START MY LIFE WITH A BRAND-NEW LEASE.
ATLANTIC CITY WITH A MALIBU BREEZE—

CARLA

AND A BRAND-NEW WEAVE—

DANIELA

OR MAYBE JUST BLEACH.

VANESSA

Y'ALL ARE FREAKS.

USNAVI

IT'S SILLY WHEN WE GET INTO THESE CRAZY HYPOTHETIC
YOU REALLY WANT SOME BREAD, THEN GO AHEAD, CREATE A ~~~
GOALS
AND CROSS THEM OFF THE LIST AS YOU PURSUE 'EM,
AND WITH THOSE NINETY-SIX I KNOW PRECISELY WHAT I'M DOIN'.

VANESSA

WHAT YOU DOIN'?

USNAVI

WHAT'M I DOIN'? WHAT'M I DOIN'?
IT TAKES MOST OF THAT CASH JUST TO SAVE MY ASS FROM FINANCIAL
RUIN.
SONNY CAN KEEP THE COFFEE BREWIN', I'LL SPEND A FEW ON YOU
'CUZ THE ONLY ROOM WITH A VIEW'S A ROOM WITH YOU IN IT.
AND I COULD GIVE ABUELA CLAUDIA THE REST OF IT.
JUST FLY ME DOWN TO PUERTA PLATA, I'LL MAKE THE BEST OF IT.
YOU REALLY LOVE THIS BUSINESS?

SONNY

NO.

USNAVI

TOUGH. MERRY CHRISTMAS!
YOU'RE NOW THE YOUNGEST TYCOON IN WASHINGTON HIZNITS.

SONNY

Yo!
WITH NINETY-SIX THOUSAND, I'D FINALLY FIX HOUSIN',
GIVE THE BARRIO COMPUTERS AND WIRELESS WEB BROWSIN'.
YOUR KIDS ARE LIVIN' WITHOUT A GOOD EDUMACATION,
CHANGE THE STATION, TEACH 'EM ABOUT GENTRIFICATION.
THE RENT IS ESCALATIN'.

GRAFFITI PETE

.?

SONNY

THE RICH ARE PENETRATIN'.

GRAFFITI PETE

WHAT?

SONNY

WE PAY OUR CORPORATIONS WHEN WE SHOULD BE DEMONSTRATIN'.

GRAFFITI PETE

WHAT?!

SONNY

WHAT ABOUT IMMIGRATION?

GRAFFITI PETE

WHAT?

SONNY

POLITICIANS BE HATIN'.

GRAFFITI PETE

WHAT?

SONNY

RACISM IN THIS NATION'S GONE FROM LATENT TO BLATANT!

GRAFFITI PETE/MEN

OOOOOH!

SONNY

I'LL CASH MY TICKET AND PICKET, INVEST IN PROTEST!
NEVER LOSE MY FOCUS TILL THE CITY TAKES NOTICE

AND YOU KNOW THIS MAN! I'LL NEVER SLEEP
BECAUSE THE GHETTO HAS A MILLION PROMISES FOR ME TO KEEP!

(*A stunned silence.* VANESSA *kisses* SONNY *on the cheek.*)

VANESSA

You are so cute!

SONNY

I was just thinking off the top of my head.

USNAVI

Ninety-six K. Go.

VANESSA

IF I WIN THE LOTTERY, YOU'LL NEVER SEE ME AGAIN.

USNAVI

DAMN, WE'RE ONLY JOKIN', STAY BROKE THEN.

VANESSA

I'LL BE DOWNTOWN,
GET A NICE STUDIO, GET OUT OF THE BARRIO.

VANESSA	BENNY
IF I WIN THE LOTTERY, YOU'LL WONDER WHERE I'VE BEEN.	FOR REAL, THOUGH. IMAGINE HOW IT WOULD FEEL GOIN' REAL SLOW DOWN THE HIGHWAY OF LIFE WITH NO REGRETS AND NO BREAKIN' YOUR NECK FOR RESPECT OR A PAYCHECK—

VANESSA	BENNY
I'LL BE DOWNTOWN,	FOR REAL, THOUGH. I'LL TAKE A BREAK FROM THE WHEEL AND WE'LL THROW
SEE YOU AROUND!	THE BIGGEST BLOCK PARTY, EVERYBODY HERE, A WEEKEND WHEN WE CAN BREATHE, TAKE IT EASY.
IF I WIN THE LOTTERY, YOU WON'T SEE A LOT OF ME!	FOR REAL THOUGH, IMAGINE HOW IT WOULD FEEL GOIN' REAL SLOW, DOWN THE HIGHWAY OF LIFE WITH NO REGRETS, AND NO BREAKIN' YOUR NECK FOR RESPECT OR A PAYCHECK

USNAVI

IT'S SILLY WHEN WE GET INTO
THESE CRAZY HYPOTHETICALS, YOU
REALLY WANT SOME BREAD, THEN
GO AHEAD, CREATE A SET OF GOALS
AND CROSS THEM OFF THE LIST AS
YOU PURSUE 'EM, AND WITH THOSE
NINETY-SIX I KNOW PRECISELY
WHAT I'M DOIN'.

IT'S SILLY WHEN WE GET INTO
THESE CRAZY HYPOTHETICALS, YOU
REALLY WANT SOME BREAD, THEN
GO AHEAD, CREATE A SET OF GOALS,
AND CROSS THEM OFF THE LIST AS
YOU PURSUE 'EM, AND WITH THOSE

NINETY-SIX I
KNOW PRECISELY
WHAT I'M DOIN'!

SONNY/DANIELA/ENSEMBLE
NINETY-SIX THOUSAND

CARLA
NO ME DIGA!

SONNY/DANIELA/ENSEMBLE
NINETY-SIX THOUSAND

CARLA
NO ME DIGA!

DANIELA
NOVENTI-SEISMIL!

SONNY/DANIELA
NO ME DIGA!

ENSEMBLE
WHY-OOH

WOMEN
CHECK
ONE, TWO, THREE

MEN
AND WITH THE DOLLAH DOLLAH

WOMEN
WITH NINETY-SIX G'S

MEN
WE GET TO HOLLAH HOLLAH

WOMEN
BETWEEN YOU AND ME

VANESSA	**BENNY**
I'LL BE DOWNTOWN,	FOR REAL THOUGH,
	I'LL TAKE A BREAK FROM THE WHEEL
	AND WE'LL THROW
SEE YOU AROUND!	THE BIGGEST BLOCK PARTY, EVERYBODY HERE,
	A WEEKEND WHEN WE CAN BREATHE,
AROUND!	TAKE IT EASY. OOH, WHOA, HO!

MEN
WE ROCK THE HOT IMPALA

ENSEMBLE
WHY-OOH

USNAVI
IT'S SILLY WHEN WE GET INTO
THESE CRAZY HYPOTHETICALS,

WOMEN/MEN
WITH NINETY-SIX G'S

MEN
WE MOVIN' ON TOMORRAH

YOU REALLY WANT SOME BREAD
THEN GO AHEAD,
CREATE A SET OF GOALS,

WOMEN
A BRAND-NEW LEASE

MEN
WE ROCK BEYOND MAÑANA,

WOMEN
A MALIBU BREEZE

AND CROSS THEM OFF THE LIST AS
YOU PURSUE 'EM,

MEN
WE DROP THE MAMA DRAMA,
WE STOP AT THE BAHAMAS!

AND WITH THOSE
NINETY-SIX

WOMEN
WHY-OH!

I KNOW PRECISELY WHAT I'M DOIN'!

MEN
WE DRINK PIÑA COLADAS!
POP 'N' LOCKIN' UP THE BLOCK

AND WITH THOSE NINETY-SIX I
KNOW PRECISELY WHAT I'M DOIN'!

WOMEN
WHO-OH!

MEN
DROP IT LIKE IT'S HOT!

WOMEN/MEN

WHO-OAA!

WHO-OAA!

VANESSA

I'LL BE DOWNTOWN!

	WOMEN/MEN
USNAVI/BENNY/SONNY	WHO-OAA!
WE COULD PAY OFF THE DEBTS WE OWE	WHO-OAA!

VANESSA/CARLA/DANIELA

WE COULD TELL EVERYONE
WE KNOW   WHO-OAA!

USNAVI

I COULD GET ON A PLANE AND GO   WHO-OAA!

USNAVI/BENNY/SONNY

WE BE SWIMMIN' IN DOUGH,
YO!

USNAVI/BENNY/SONNY/OTHERS

NO TIP-TOEIN'   WHO-OAA!
WE'LL GET THE DOUGH 'N'

ALL

ONCE WE GET GOIN'
WE NEVER GONNA
STOP TIP-TOEIN'
WE'LL GET THE DOUGH AN'
ONCE WE GET GOIN',
WE'RE NEVER GONNA—

BENNY/CARLA/ DANIELA/OTHERS	ENSEMBLE	USNAVI/SONNY/ GRAFFITI PETE
NINETY-SIX THOUSAND	WE'LL GET THE	WHA'?
NINETY-SIX THOUSAND	DOUGH 'N'	WHA'?
NINETY-SIX THOUSAND	ONCE WE GET GOIN'	WHA'?
		WHA'?

ALL

WE'LL GET THE DOUGH 'N'
ONCE WE GET GOIN'
WE'RE NEVER GONNA STOP!

"96,000 Playoff"

ALL

NINETY-SIX THOUSAND—
NINETY-SIX THOUSAND—
NINETY-SIX THOUSAND—

SCENE 8

(*The street.* NINA *and* CAMILA *enter.*)

CAMILA

Call your father. He was supposed to help me, and he's not picking up.

NINA

We're fine, we have all afternoon.

CAMILA

We are not fine.

(*They exit into the bodega.* ABUELA CLAUDIA *comes out onto her stoop.*)

ABUELA CLAUDIA

Ay, que calor. Usnavi, ooo-oo!

(USNAVI *enters.*)

USNAVI

Something's wrong, you were off-pitch.

ABUELA CLAUDIA

It's the heat. Toma, your ham and cheese.

USNAVI

Thanks. You know, you already brought me one.

ABUELA CLAUDIA

De verdad? My memory goes two miles an hour. I'm taking a walk, I need some air.

USNAVI

Breadcrumbs for your birds. (*Hands* ABUELA CLAUDIA *a little bag.*) Stay in the shade, okay?

ABUELA CLAUDIA

Ah! I should stop by Padre Carlos's church and light a few candles.

USNAVI

Light one for my busted grate. I gotta go call the mechanic about that thing. Mi amor, like you always say, patience and faith.

ABUELA CLAUDIA

Paciencia y fe.

"Paciencia y Fe"

ABUELA CLAUDIA

CALOR . . . CALOR . . . CALOR . . .
CALOR . . . CALOR . . . CALOR . . .

AY, MAMÁ!
THE SUMMER'S HOTTEST DAY!
PACIENCIA Y FE! PACIENCIA Y FE!
AY, CARAJO, IT'S HOT!

(She makes the sign of the cross.)

BUT THAT'S OKAY!
MAMÁ WOULD SAY, "PACIENCIA Y FE!"
IT WAS HOTTER AT HOME IN LA VÍBORA
THE WASHINGTON HEIGHTS OF HAVANA!
A CROWDED CITY OF FACES THE SAME AS MINE!
BACK AS A CHILD IN LA VÍBORA
I CHASED THE BIRDS IN THE PLAZA
PRAYING, MAMÁ, YOU WOULD FIND WORK.
COMBING THE STARS IN THE SKY FOR SOME SORT OF SIGN!
AY, MAMÁ! SO MANY STARS IN CUBA.
EN NUEVA YORK WE CAN'T SEE BEYOND OUR STREETLIGHTS!
TO REACH THE ROOF YOU GOTTA BRIBE THE SUPA!
AIN'T NO CASSIOPEIA IN WASHINGTON HEIGHTS.
BUT AIN'T NO FOOD IN LA VÍBORA . . .

I REMEMBER NIGHTS, ANGER IN THE STREETS, HUNGER AT THE WINDOWS
WOMEN FOLDING CLOTHES, PLAYING WITH MY FRIENDS IN THE SUMMER
RAIN.
MAMÁ NEEDS A JOB, MAMÁ SAYS WE'RE POOR, ONE DAY YOU SAY
"VAMOS A NUEVA YORK."
AND NUEVA YORK WAS FAR, BUT NUEVA YORK HAD WORK AND SO WE
CAME.

AND NOW, I'M WIDE AWAKE
A MILLION YEARS TOO LATE.
I TALK TO YOU, IMAGINING WHAT YOU'D DO,
REMEMBERING WHAT WE WENT THROUGH . . .

(The music swells into a mambo groove. Passersby on the sidewalk come
to life, waving hello to ABUELA CLAUDIA *as they pass.)*

ACT 1

NUEVA YORK! AY, MAMÁ!
IT WASN'T LIKE TODAY.
YOU'D SAY,
"PACIENCIA Y FE."

ENSEMBLE (PIRAGUA GUY/WOMEN/MEN)
PACIENCIA Y FE.

ABUELA CLAUDIA
PACIENCIA Y FE.

ENSEMBLE
PACIENCIA Y—

ABUELA CLAUDIA
FRESH OFF THE BOAT IN AMERICA,
FREEZING IN EARLY DECEMBER.
A CROWDED CITY IN NINETEEN FORTY-THREE!
LEARNING THE ROPES IN AMERICA.
EN ESPAÑOL, I REMEMBER
DANCING WITH MAYOR LAGUARDIA.
ALL OF SOCIETY WELCOMING MAMI AND ME.
HA!

ENSEMBLE + BACKGROUND (NINA/USNAVI/OTHERS)
YOU BETTER CLEAN THIS MESS!

ABUELA CLAUDIA
PACIENCIA Y FE . . .

ENSEMBLE + BACKGROUND
YOU BETTER LEARN INGLÉS!

ABUELA CLAUDIA
PACIENCIA Y FE . . .

ENSEMBLE + BACKGROUND
YOU BETTER NOT BE LATE.

YOU BETTER PULL YOUR WEIGHT!
ARE YOU BETTER OFF THAN YOU WERE WITH THE BIRDS OF LA VÍBORA?

ABUELA CLAUDIA

SHARING DOUBLE BEDS, TRYING TO CATCH A BREAK, STRUGGLING WITH ENGLISH.
LISTENING TO FRIENDS, FINALLY GOT A JOB WORKING AS A MAID.
SO WE CLEANED SOME HOMES, POLISHING WITH PRIDE, SCRUBBING THE WHOLE OF THE UPPER EAST SIDE,
THE DAYS INTO WEEKS, THE WEEKS INTO YEARS, AND HERE I STAYED.

USNAVI/BENNY/GRAFFITI PETE/MAN

PACIENCIA Y FE . . .

SONNY/PIRAGUA GUY/TWO MEN

PACIENCIA Y FE . . .

MEN + DANIELA/NINA/OTHERS

PACIENCIA Y FE . . .

ABUELA CLAUDIA	USNAVI/NINA/OTHERS + OFFSTAGE GROUP
AND AS I FEED THESE BIRDS,	
MY HANDS BEGIN TO SHAKE—	OOH,
AND AS I SAY THESE WORDS,	OOH, OOH,
MY HEART'S ABOUT TO BREAK.	AND AY MAMÁ!
AND AY MAMÁ,	
WHAT DO YOU DO WHEN YOUR	
DREAMS COME TRUE?	AND AY MAMÁ!
I'VE SPENT MY LIFE	AAH, AH!
INHERITING	
DREAMS FROM YOU.	

(ABUELA CLAUDIA *holds up a lottery ticket.*)

ABUELA CLAUDIA

WHAT DO I DO WITH THIS WINNING TICKET?
WHAT CAN I DO BUT PRAY?

I BUY MY LOAF OF BREAD.
CONTINUE WITH MY DAY.
AND SEE YOU IN MY HEAD,
IMAGINING WHAT YOU'D SAY.
THE BIRDS, THEY FLY AWAY,
DO THEY FLY TO LA VÍBORA?

(*She stops and laughs.*)

Alright, Mamá. Okay.

PACIENCIA Y FE.

USNAVI/NINA/OTHERS + OFFSTAGE GROUP
CALOR, CALOR, CALOR!

SCENE 9

(*Early evening.* NINA *at* ABUELA CLAUDIA*'s stoop. She rings the
doorbell, no answer. She knocks on the door, no answer.* SONNY *enters
from the bodega.*)

SONNY
Well, well, well. Nina Rosario. I think we both know what time it is.

NINA
Your bedtime?

SONNY
Not yet, it's time you open that wounded soul up to Sonny.

NINA
It's tempting.

SONNY
You need a welcome-home slushie. Two parts blue raspberry, one part cherry
cola, and check this out. I mix in some Nerds at the end . . . mm!

(BENNY *enters from the dispatch*.)

BENNY

(*Calling behind him.*) Domingo, it's all you.

NINA

(*To* SONNY.) Can I get a rain check on that slushie?

SONNY

But—

BENNY

Yo, Sonny. (*Gestures that* SONNY *should get lost.*)

SONNY

One day you'll both need my sympathy and will I be there? Probably.

(*He exits.*)

BENNY

Is this step taken?

NINA

(*Scoots over.*) Did you learn some more curse words?

BENNY

(*Sits.*) I'm trying but it's like two different languages. Dominican Spanish, Puerto Rican Spanish.

NINA

I hear you. They spoke a different kind of English at Stanford.

BENNY

Really?

NINA

"Weekend." Verb. To go skiing at your cabin on Lake Tahoe. "Cabin." Noun. A blasé word for mansion.

BENNY

Well, did you teach them a few words from home?

NINA

Of course. "Would you like some fries with that?"

BENNY

(*Like a toast.*) To not speaking the language.

"When You're Home"

NINA

I USED TO THINK WE LIVED AT THE TOP OF THE WORLD,
WHEN THE WORLD WAS JUST A SUBWAY MAP.
AND THE ONE SLASH NINE CLIMBED A DOTTED LINE TO MY PLACE.

BENNY

THERE'S NO NINE TRAIN NOW.

NINA

RIGHT.
I USED TO THINK THE BRONX WAS A PLACE IN THE SKY,
WHEN THE WORLD WAS JUST A SUBWAY MAP.
AND MY THOUGHTS TOOK SHAPE

NINA/BENNY

ON THAT FIRE ESCAPE . . .

NINA

CAN YOU REMIND ME OF WHAT IT WAS LIKE
AT THE TOP OF THE WORLD?

BENNY

COME WITH ME.
WE BEGIN JULY
WITH A STOP AT MY CORNER FIRE HYDRANT.

NINA

YOU WOULD OPEN IT EVERY SUMMER!

BENNY

I WOULD BUST IT WITH A WRENCH
TILL MY FACE GOT DRENCHED,
TILL I HEARD THE SIRENS.
THEN I RAN LIKE HELL!

NINA

YOU RAN LIKE HELL!

BENNY

YEAH, I RAN LIKE HELL!

NINA

I REMEMBER WELL!

BENNY

TO YOUR FATHER'S DISPATCH WINDOW,

(*He bangs on the window.*)

"HEY, LET ME IN, YO!
THEY'RE COMING TO GET ME!"

NINA

YOU WERE ALWAYS IN CONSTANT TROUBLE—

BENNY

THEN YOUR DAD WOULD ACT ALL SNIDE, BUT HE LET ME HIDE
YOU'D BE THERE INSIDE—

NINA

LIFE WAS EASIER THEN.

BENNY

NINA, EVERYTHING IS EASIER

WHEN YOU'RE HOME . . .
THE STREET'S A LITTLE KINDER WHEN YOU'RE HOME.
CAN'T YOU SEE
THAT THE DAY SEEMS CLEARER
NOW THAT YOU ARE HERE, OR
IS IT ME?
MAYBE IT'S JUST ME . . .

WE GOTTA GO, I WANNA SHOW YOU ALL I KNOW.
THE SUN IS SETTING AND THE LIGHT IS GETTING LOW.

NINA
ARE WE GOING TO CASTLE GARDEN?

BENNY
MAYBE, MAYBE NOT, BUT WAY TO TAKE A SHOT, WHEN THE DAY IS HOT
I GOT A PERFECT SHADY SPOT A LITTLE WAYS AWAY THAT OUGHTA
COOL US DOWN.

NINA
COOL US DOWN—

BENNY
WELCOME BACK TO TOWN!

NINA
NOW, BACK IN HIGH SCHOOL WHEN IT DARKENED
YOU'D HANG OUT IN BENNETT PARK AND—

BENNY
USNAVI WOULD BRING HIS RADIO!

NINA
AS I WALKED HOME FROM SENIOR STUDIES,
I'D SEE YOU RAPPING WITH YOUR BUDDIES.

BENNY
WITH THE VOLUME HIGH—

NINA

I WALKED ON BY!

BENNY

YOU WALKED ON BY—

(*A cluster of guys enter, listening to a boom box.*)

USNAVI/GRAFFITI PETE/TWO MEN	DANIELA/CARLA/SONNY/OTHERS
NO PARE SIGUE SIGUE!	WHOAA
NO PARE SIGUE SIGUE!	OH!
NO PARE SIGUE SIGUE!	WHOAA
NO PARE SIGUE SIGUE!	OH!
NO PARE SIGUE SIGUE!	WHOAA
NO PARE SIGUE SIGUE!	OH!
NO PARE SIGUE SIGUE!	WHOAA
NO PARE SIGUE!	OH!

BENNY + ENSEMBLE (BOTH GROUPS)

WHEN YOU'RE HOME!

BENNY

OH, THE SUMMER NIGHTS ARE COOLER

BENNY + ENSEMBLE

WHEN YOU'RE HOME!

NINA

NOW THAT YOU'RE HERE WITH ME . . .

BENNY		ENSEMBLE
AND THAT SONG YOU'RE	OOH	
HEARING IS THE	OOH	
NEIGHBORHOOD JUST CHEERING	OOH	
YOU ALONG—	OOH.	

NINA

DON'T SAY THAT.

BENNY

WHAT'S WRONG?

NINA

DON'T SAY THAT!
WHEN I WAS YOUNGER, I'D IMAGINE WHAT WOULD HAPPEN
IF MY PARENTS HAD STAYED IN PUERTO RICO.
WHO WOULD I BE IF I HAD NEVER SEEN MANHATTAN,
IF I LIVED IN PUERTO RICO WITH MY PEOPLE.
MY PEOPLE?
I FEEL LIKE ALL MY LIFE I'VE TRIED TO FIND THE ANSWER.
WORKING HARDER, LEARNING SPANISH, LEARNING ALL I CAN.
I THOUGHT I MIGHT FIND THE ANSWERS OUT AT STANFORD,
BUT I'D STARE OUT AT THE SEA
THINKING, WHERE'M I SUPPOSED TO BE?
SO PLEASE DON'T SAY YOU'RE PROUD OF ME, WHEN I'VE LOST MY WAY.

BENNY

THEN CAN I SAY:
I COULDN'T GET MY MIND OFF YOU ALL DAY.
NOW LISTEN TO ME!
THAT MAY BE HOW YOU PERCEIVE IT,
BUT, NINA, PLEASE BELIEVE
THAT WHEN YOU FIND YOUR WAY AGAIN,
YOU ARE GONNA CHANGE THE WORLD AND THEN
WE'RE ALL GONNA BRAG AND SAY, "WE KNEW HER WHEN!"
THIS WAS YOUR HOME.

NINA

I'M HOME—

BENNY

WELCOME HOME—

NINA

WHEN YOU'RE HERE WITH ME—

                    BENNY
WELCOME HOME—

                    NINA
I USED TO THINK WE LIVED AT THE TOP OF THE WORLD.

                    BENNY
WELCOME HOME—

                    NINA
I'M HOME—

          BENNY   **NINA**
YOU'RE FINALLY HOME.   I'M HOME—
YOU'RE HOME!   I'M HOME!

(*Sun sets on the neighborhood.*)

SCENE 10

(*Dusk, neighbors fan themselves on stoops.* PIRAGUA GUY *scrapes from his ice block.*)

"Piragua"

                    PIRAGUA GUY
AY, QUE CALOR, QUE CALOR, QUE CALOR, QUE CALO-O-OR!

PIRAGUA, PIRAGUA,
NEW BLOCK OF ICE, PIRAGUA!
PIRAGUA, PIRAGUA,
SO SWEET AND NICE, PIRAGUA!

TENGO DE MANGO, TENGO DE PARCHA,
DE PIÑA Y DE FRESA!

TENGO DE CHINA, DE LIMÓN,
DE PESO Y DE PESETA, AY!

PIRAGUA, PIRAGUA,
NEW BLOCK OF ICE, PIRAGUA!
PIRAGUA, PIRAGUA,
SO SWEET AND NICE, PIRAGUA!

IT'S HOTTER THAN THE ISLANDS ARE TONIGHT.
AND MR. SOFTEE'S TRYING TO SHUT ME DOWN.
BUT I KEEP SCRAPING BY THE FADING LIGHT.
HEY, 'PANA, THIS IS MY TOWN!

PIRAGUA, PIRAGUA,
KEEP SCRAPING BY, PIRAGUA!

PIRAGUA, PIRAGUA,
KEEP SCRAPING BY, PIRAGUA!

KEEP SCRAPING BY, KEEP SCRAPING BY,
LAI LO LE LO LAI, LAI LO LE LO LAI!

KEEP SCRAPING BY, KEEP SCRAPING BY,
LAI LO LE LO LAI!

KEEP SCRAPING BY . . .

QUE CALOR, QUE CALOR, QUE CALOR, QUE CALO-O-OR!

SCENE 11

(*The Rosario household. An old record plays.* NINA *and* CAMILA *dance.* VANESSA *dances up to* ABUELA CLAUDIA.)

VANESSA

Yo, tomorrow's the Fourth of July, it's time to party! Come on, Abuela Claudia, I'll show you some new moves.

ABUELA CLAUDIA

Vamos, but no bump and grind!

(*They dance.*)

CAMILA

(*Pulls* NINA *to dance.*) It's my song . . .

NINA

We really don't have to.

CAMILA

Yes we do. I dance best when I'm angry.

(*They dance.*)

ABUELA CLAUDIA

(*To* VANESSA.) It's too much nalgas. Be subtle. Pretend you're dancing on a tiny brick.

VANESSA

Uh-uh, Abuela, I shake my ass!

CAMILA

(*Singing along to the record.*) NO TE VAYAS!
SI ME DEJAS,
SI TE ALEJAS DE MI,
SEGUIRAS EN MIS RECUERDOS PARA SIEMPRE—

(*The record hits a skip.*)

PARA SIEMPRE . . . PARA SIEMPRE . . .

(*She turns off the record.*)

The scratch in the record is my favorite part!

(USNAVI *enters.*)

USNAVI

Damn, did we miss the record scratch?

(BENNY *enters*.)

BENNY

Put the music back on!

CAMILA

Bueno, but no encores! Show up late, you miss the hot stuff!

USNAVI

New Zealand Shiraz. Vintage 2008.

BENNY

Some pastel de guava for dessert.

USNAVI

(*To* CLAUDIA.) Bendición.

ABUELA CLAUDIA

Que Dios te bendiga! Alabanza to the day! We have to talk later . . .

USNAVI

So, West Village, do I owe you a bottle of champagne?

VANESSA

The landlord saw my credit application and laughed. Out loud.

NINA

Screw him. It wasn't the right place for you.

VANESSA

No, there was exposed brick on purpose, not because the walls were all busted.

NINA

Don't worry about that. We should all go dancing later . . .

BENNY

If there's A.C., I'm there. (*To* USNAVI.) You in?

USNAVI

Actually, Vanessa and I already have plans.

VANESSA

Yeah, come with us. The more friends the better, right?

USNAVI

You know it, friend!

(KEVIN *enters*.)

KEVIN

The West Side Highway was bumper to bumper!

CAMILA

There you are!

BENNY

Boss, how's it going?

USNAVI

El jefe!

VANESSA

What's up, Mr. Rosario?

ABUELA CLAUDIA

Mira pa'lla. Who's that handsome man?

KEVIN

(*Kisses* ABUELA CLAUDIA.) It's my beautiful princesa.

NINA

Hey, Dad . . .

KEVIN

(*To* NINA.) Excuse me. You're the princess, Claudia is the queen.

CAMILA

And what does that make me?

KEVIN

The dictator.

(KEVIN *and* CAMILA *kiss.*)

CAMILA

Damn straight! One day I'll open my Restaurante Boricua. Until then, you're all my guinea pigs! Serve yourselves, plates are in the kitchen!

KEVIN

Listen up, everyone. Atención!

CAMILA

Let's serve first, the food is gonna get cold.

KEVIN

Cami, the pernil can wait five minutes. (*He clears his throat.*) Twenty-seven years ago in Arecibo, Puerto Rico, I threw down my shovel, hitched a ride into town, and bought two plane tickets to Nueva Yol. I showed up at Camila's house with a suitcase and said vamos.

CAMILA

That whole plane ride I was trying not to cry, verdad?

KEVIN

That whole plane ride you were drinking Bacardi.

CAMILA

Sin vergüenza!

KEVIN

We were Nina's age. (*To* NINA.) And now look at you. You make me proud to be

Lin-Manuel Miranda (Usnavi)

Lin-Manuel Miranda (Usnavi) and company in "In The Heights"

Karen Olivo (Vanessa) in "It Won't Be Long Now"

Olga Merediz (Abuela Claudia) and Mandy Gonzalez (Nina)

Robin De Jesús (Sonny), Karen Olivo (Vanessa), and Lin-Manuel Miranda (Usnavi) in "It Won't Be Long Now"

Janet Dacal (Carla) and Andréa Burns (Daniela) in "No Me Diga"

Lin-Manuel Miranda (Usnavi), Robin De Jesús (Sonny), Christopher Jackson (Benny), and company in "96,000"

Andréa Burns (Daniela) and company (including Luis Salgado, kneeling) in "Carnaval Del Barrio"

a Rosario. So today I threw down my shovel again. I hitched a ride into town. I took another leap of faith. Nina, I sold the business to pay for your tuition.

NINA

What?

KEVIN

I sold Rosario's. You're going back to Stanford.

CAMILA

Kevin, this had better be a joke.

KEVIN

Uptown Investment takes over in two weeks.

CAMILA

Uptown? Ay Dios mio, they offered us nothing!

KEVIN

It was enough, mi vida.

NINA

Wait. Dad, I'll find a job. I can take night classes!

KEVIN

What, so you end up just another girl stuck in el barrio?

VANESSA

Why you gotta look at me when you say that?

BENNY

Hold up, did I just lose my job?

CAMILA

Of course you didn't. (*To* KEVIN.) I do the payroll, the banking, your chaotic papers. We worked twenty years to build this company. I worked!

KEVIN

For what, Cami? Twenty years for what?

NINA

What about your employees?

BENNY

You can't just kick us to the curb.

USNAVI

Your drivers are half my customers.

KEVIN

I'm not a welfare office! Family comes first, above everything.

BENNY

The day you hired me you said I was family.

KEVIN

That's business. This is my daughter.

CAMILA

You are all my family, and you have my word: we are not selling Rosario's.

KEVIN

I'm making the damn deal.

CAMILA

This is our business!

KEVIN

It was in my name!

CAMILA

Dinner is over.

(*She exits.*)

NINA

Mom!

VANESSA

Excuse me. I'm not good enough to sit with the bourgeoisie. (VANESSA *exits.*)

ABUELA CLAUDIA

Con permiso.

USNAVI

Vente, Abuela.

(USNAVI *and* ABUELA CLAUDIA *exit.*)

NINA

(*To* BENNY.) Benny, I'll fix this, I promise—

KEVIN

Nina, stay away from him!

BENNY

(*To* KEVIN.) I'll get out of your way.

(*He exits.* NINA *and* KEVIN *are alone.*)

NINA

You know I will never touch that money.

KEVIN

So help me God, you are flying back to California.

(NINA *exits.*)

Nina!

SCENE 12

(*The club.* VANESSA *enters.* USNAVI *follows.* BENNY *is drinking at the bar.*)

"The Club"

CLUB PEOPLE

VANESSA!

(USNAVI *tries to keep up with her.*)

USNAVI

DAMN, THIS IS NICE.
I REALLY LIKE WHAT THEY'VE DONE WITH THE LIGHTS.
SO, THE HOT CLUB IN WASHINGTON HEIGHTS.
YOU MIGHT BE RIGHT, THIS MUSIC'S TIGHT,
YO, DID I MENTION THAT YOU LOOK GREAT TONIGHT?
BECAUSE YOU DO, YOU REALLY—

VANESSA

USNAVI, RELAX!

USNAVI

RELAX. QUE RELAXED? I'M RELAXED!

(*A couple dances by.*)

MAN/WOMAN

WEPA! VANESSA!

USNAVI

SO, YOU'VE BEEN HERE BEFORE.
I DON'T GO OUT. I GET SO BUSY WITH THE STORE.
Y CADA DÍA, IT'S A BRAND-NEW CHORE,
MY ARMS ARE SORE, NO TIME FOR THE DANCE FLOOR!
BUT MAYBE YOU AND ME SHOULD HANG OUT SOME MORE.

I'M SUCH A DORK, BUT I—

VANESSA

LET'S GO GET A DRINK.

USNAVI

SOMETHING SWEET.

VANESSA

YOU KNOW ME. A LITTLE BIT OF CINNAMON.

ALL

WEPA! VANESSA!

(USNAVI *joins* BENNY *at the bar.* BENNY *is doing shots.*)

BENNY

HERE'S TO GETTING FIRED!

USNAVI

TO KILLING THE MOOD!

BOTH

SALUD!

(*They do a shot.*)

BENNY

WITHOUT SO MUCH AS A THANK-YOU!

USNAVI

AFTER ALL THESE YEARS.

BOTH

CHEERS!

(*They do another shot.*)

TO FINALLY GETTING VANESSA,
MAN, FIX YOUR COLLAR—

(*He fixes* USNAVI*'s collar.*)

USNAVI/BENNY

HOLLER!

BENNY

TO DOING SHOTS ON A WEEKEND!

USNAVI

AS LONG AS YOU BUY 'EM, L'CHAIM!

(*Another shot. A* CLUB GUY *approaches* VANESSA.)

CLUB GUY

HEY, YOU!

VANESSA

WHO?

CLUB GUY

YOU!

VANESSA

WHO, ME?

CLUB GUY

YOU WANNA DANCE?

VANESSA

NAW, MAN.

CLUB GUY

OKAY, I TOOK MY CHANCE!

USNAVI

IT'S COOL, IT'S COOL, HEY, IF YOU WANT TO!

VANESSA

YOU DON'T MIND?

USNAVI

I'M FINE! I'M FINE!

BENNY

YO!

USNAVI

YO!

BENNY

WHO'S VANESSA TALKIN' TO?

USNAVI

SOME DUDE.

BENNY

SOME DUDE?!
THAT'S MESSED UP, SHE'S TRYIN' TO MAKE YOU JEALOUS!

USNAVI

JEALOUS, I AIN'T JEALOUS! I CAN TAKE ALL THESE FELLAS, WHATEVER!

(USNAVI *grabs* VANESSA *from* CLUB GUY *and dances with her.* CLUB GUY *is pissed.* NINA *enters.*)

NINA

BENNY, CAN WE TAKE A WALK OUTSIDE?

BENNY

AND THERE SHE IS.

NINA

I'M SO SORRY. I DIDN'T KNOW.

BENNY

WHO LET YOU IN? THIS IS THE GIRL WHO COST US OUR JOBS TODAY!

NINA

I'M GONNA MAKE IT RIGHT!

(BENNY *raises his glass to* NINA.)

BENNY

A TOAST TO THE END OF ALL I KNOW!

NINA

YOU'VE HAD ENOUGH.

BENNY

SAYS THE GIRL WHO HAS IT ALL.

NINA

THAT'S NOT FAIR.

BENNY

WELL, WHY DON'T YOU RUN HOME TO DADDY?
HE LOVES TO REMIND ME THAT I'LL NEVER BE GOOD ENOUGH FOR YOUR
FAMILY. FOR YOU.

NINA

YOU DON'T KNOW ME.

BENNY

POOR YOU.

NINA

I THOUGHT YOU WERE DIFFERENT.

(BENNY *shoves his drink in* NINA*'s hand and pulls* CLUB GIRL 1 *to the dance floor.*)

BENNY

SALUD!
Come on.

(*A chorus of boys swoops in on* VANESSA, *stealing her from* USNAVI, *alternating as they swing her around the floor.*)

PIRAGUA GUY/GRAFFITI PETE/MEN

VANESSA, LET ME GET THE NEXT ONE!
VANESSA, LET ME INTERJECT SOME!
THE WAY YOU SWEAT, THE WAY YOU FLEX ON THE FLOOR,
IT MAKES ME WANT YOU MORE!

VANESSA, LET ME GET THE NEXT ONE!
VANESSA, LET ME INTERJECT SOME!
THE WAY YOU SWEAT, THE WAY YOU FLEX ON THE FLOOR,
IT MAKES ME WANT YOU MORE!

VANESSA, LET ME GET THE NEXT ONE!
VANESSA, LET ME INTERJECT SOME!
THE WAY YOU SWEAT, THE WAY YOU FLEX ON THE FLOOR,
IT MAKES ME WANT YOU MORE!

(USNAVI *approaches* CLUB GIRL 2 *at the bar.*)

USNAVI

BARTENDER!
LET ME GET AN AMARETTO SOUR FOR THIS GHETTO FLOWER.
HOW ARE YOU SO PRETTY?
YOU COMPLETE ME.
YOU HAD ME AT HELLO, YOU KNOW YOU NEED ME,
TRULY, MADLY, DEEPLY, LET'S GET FREAKY.
OH, I GET IT, YOU'RE THE STRONG AND SILENT TYPE!
WELL, I'M THE CARIBBEAN ISLAND TYPE

AND I CAN DRIVE YOU WILD ALL NIGHT!
BUT I DIGRESS,
SAY SOMETHING SO I DON'T STRESS.

CLUB GIRL 2

NO HABLO INGLÉS.

USNAVI

YES!

(USNAVI *takes her out on the floor. Everyone is dancing.* VANESSA *and* CLUB GUY. USNAVI *and* CLUB GIRL 2. BENNY *and* CLUB GIRL 1. NINA *finds another guy to dance with and spins by* BENNY. BENNY *is pissed.* USNAVI *swoops in and takes* VANESSA *out of* CLUB GUY's *hands and dances with her.* CLUB GUY, *without missing a beat, glides back in and takes* VANESSA *back, mid-turn. To add insult to injury, he grabs* CLUB GIRL 2, *and is now dipping and spinning them both on the dance floor. During this impressive display,* USNAVI *and a very drunk* BENNY *slide in and each grab a girl, leaving* CLUB GUY *dancing alone.* CLUB GUY, *angry, starts to tap* USNAVI *on the shoulder. Without missing a beat,* BENNY *hauls and punches* CLUB GUY *across the face. More and more instruments add to the mix. The dancing gets intense, crazy. It is a whirlwind of movement, a release of stress, when suddenly:*

THE POWER GOES OUT IN WASHINGTON HEIGHTS.

Complete darkness. A cell phone light appears, illuminating a face. More and more cell phones light up, creating a blue glow in the club.)

"Blackout"

(*A flashlight comes on in the dispatch booth.*)

PIRAGUA GUY

OYE QUÉ PASÓ?

USNAVI

BLACKOUT, BLACKOUT!

PIRAGUA GUY	**GRAFFITI PETE/MEN**
VINO EL APAGÓN AY DIOS!	OH, NO!

PIRAGUA GUY/		**GRAFFITI PETE/**
TWO MEN	**USNAVI**	**DANIELA/CARLA/**
		OTHERS
OYE QUÉ PASÓ?	BLACKOUT, BLACKOUT!	OH, NO!

PIRAGUA GUY/		
TWO MEN	**BENNY**	**ENSEMBLE**
VINO EL APAGÓN AY	HOLD UP, WAIT, HOLD	OH, NO!
DIOS!	UP, WAIT!	

USNAVI	**BENNY**	**ENSEMBLE**
YO! I! CAN'T SEE	NINA, WHERE'D YOU	OH, NO!
QUIT SHOVIN'	GO, I CAN'T FIND YOU—	
YOU SON OF A—		OH, NO!
IT'S AN OVEN	NINA, TAKE IT SLOW,	
AND WE GOTTA	I'M BEHIND YOU—	OH, NO!
BACK OUT!		
THIS IS A BLACKOUT!		OH, NO!
CHILL, FOR REAL,		
OR WE'RE GONNA GET		
KILLED!		

(*A flashlight at the bodega.* SONNY *appears outside, holding a baseball bat, protecting the storefront.*)

KEVIN	SONNY	
CALLING ALL TAXIS!	WHAT'S GOING ON?	**MEN**
KEVIN/USNAVI	WHAT'S GOING ON?	OH, NO!
EVERYONE RELAX	SUDDENLY I FIND	
PLEASE.	THE ELECTRICITY IS	OH, NO!
	GONE.	
KEVIN	WHAT'S GOING ON?	OH, NO!
CALLING ALL TAXIS!	WHAT'S GOING ON?	
		OH, NO!
KEVIN/USNAVI	I GOTTA GUARD THE	
EVERYONE RELAX	STORE MAKE SURE	
PLEASE.	THAT NOTHING'S	
	GOING WRONG!	

BENNY	SONNY	ENSEMBLE
SOMEBODY BETTER	WHAT'S GOING ON?	OH, NO!
OPEN THESE	WHAT'S GOING ON?	
GODDAMN DOORS!		

VANESSA		
SOMEBODY BETTER	GOTTA FIND USNAVI	OH, NO!
OPEN THESE	TELL HIM WHAT IS	
GODDAMN DOORS!	GOING ON	

BENNY		
SOMEBODY BETTER	NOTHING IS ON!	
OPEN THESE	NOTHING IS ON!	OH, NO!
GODDAMN DOORS!		

VANESSA		
AND I CAN'T FIND	AND I CAN'T FIND	NO! NO!
USNAVI . . .	USNAVI . . .	NO!

BENNY	USNAVI	NINA
NINA, WHERE'D YOU GO?	VANESSA,	HAS ANYONE SEEN BENNY?
NINA, WHERE'D YOU GO?	VANESSA,	
NINA, WHERE'D YOU GO?	VANESSA,	BENNY . . .

VANESSA

USNAVI,
HELP ME!

BENNY	USNAVI	NINA
I CAN'T FIND YOU!	I GOTTA GO . . .	

BENNY	USNAVI	NINA
NINA, WHERE'D YOU GO?	VANESSA,	HAS ANYONE SEEN BENNY?
NINA, WHERE'D YOU GO?	VANESSA,	
NINA, WHERE'D YOU GO?	VANESSA,	BENNY . . .
I CAN'T FIND YOU!	I GOTTA GO . . .	

USNAVI,
HELP ME!

KEVIN

PLEASE FIND NINA!
FIND CAMILA!
IF YOU SEE MY FAMILY,
BRING THEM HOME!

VANESSA

FIND MY WAY HOME—

USNAVI, HELP ME!

SONNY

WE ARE POWERLESS
WE ARE POWERLESS

YOU LEFT ME ALONE!

SONNY/CAMILA/PIRAGUA GUY/OTHERS

WE ARE POWERLESS
WE ARE POWERLESS!

GRAFFITI PETE

YO! YO! THEY THROWIN' BOTTLES IN THE STREET!
PEOPLE LOOTIN' AND SHOOTIN'.
SONNY, THEY WANNA SEE A ROBBERY,
WE GOTTA KEEP MOVIN'!

SONNY

NAW, MAN, I CAN'T LEAVE. WE GOTTA GUARD THE STORE!

GRAFFITI PETE

THEY GONNA BOMBARD THE STORE UNTIL YOU AIN'T GOT A STORE NO MORE!

SONNY

I GOT A BASEBALL BAT ON A RACK IN THE BACK.

GRAFFITI PETE

(*Opening a book bag.*) I GOT A COUPLE ROMAN CANDLES, WE CAN DISTRACT THE VANDALS!

SONNY

HEY YO, I SEE SOME THUGS COMIN'. MAN, WE GONNA GET JACKED UP!

(GRAFFITI PETE *rushes out of the store holding a Roman candle,* SONNY *behind him wielding a bat.*)

GRAFFITI PETE

GIMME A LIGHT, I'LL BE RIGHT BACK. BACK UP—

GRAFFITI PETE/SONNY

BACK UP! BACK UP!

(*We hear an explosion.*)

USNAVI/NINA/ABUELA CLAUDIA/ OTHERS	**VANESSA/DANIELA/PIRAGUA GUY/ OTHERS**
LOOK AT THE FIREWORKS!	LOOK AT THE FIREWORKS!
	LOOK AT THE FIREWORKS FLY!
LIGHT UP THE NIGHT SKY!	
	LIGHT UP THE NIGHT SKY!
LOOK AT THE FIREWORKS!	
	LOOK AT THE FIREWORKS FLY!
LIGHT UP THE NIGHT SKY!	
	LIGHT UP THE NIGHT SKY!

SONNY

IT'S LATE AND THIS GRATE WON'T COME DOWN!
COME DOWN!

SONNY	**CARLA**	**DANIELA**	**TWO MEN**
IT'S LATE AND THIS GRATE WON'T COME DOWN!	OH GOD, SO MUCH PANIC! THE CROWD WAS MANIC WITH EVERYBODY		
WE ARE POWERLESS, WE ARE POWERLESS.	SCREAMING AND SHOVING AND SHOUTING AND SLAPPING AND EVERYONE'S FRANTIC! WHAT'S HAPPENING WITH YOU?	MIRA MI AMOR, HAZME UN FAVOR. DESPIERTALE ABUELA Y A LO MEJOR ELLA TIENE UNA VELA.	WE ARE POWERLESS! WE ARE POWERLESS! **+ PIRAGUA GUY/ TWO MEN**
WE ARE POWERLESS,	WE ARE POWERLESS!	ESTUVE BAILANDO CUANDO VINO	WE ARE POWERLESS! **+ VANESSA/ TWO WOMEN**
WE ARE POWERLESS! POWERLESS!	WE ARE POWERLESS!	EL APAGÓN, AQUÍ HAY GENTE PERO NO SE QUIENES SON!	WE ARE POWERLESS! POWERLESS!

(*More explosions.* USNAVI *enters his apartment.*)

ENSEMBLE

LOOK AT THE FIREWORKS!

USNAVI

ABUELA, ARE YOU ALRIGHT?

ENSEMBLE

LIGHT UP THE NIGHT SKY!

ABUELA CLAUDIA

THE STARS ARE OUT TONIGHT!

ENSEMBLE

LOOK AT THE FIREWORKS!

USNAVI

YOU'RE NOT ALONE TONIGHT.

ENSEMBLE

LIGHT UP THE NIGHT SKY!

USNAVI/ABUELA CLAUDIA

YOU'RE/I'M NOT ALONE TONIGHT.

ABUELA CLAUDIA

USNAVI, PLEASE PROMISE ME YOU'LL GUARD THIS WITH YOUR LIFE.

(*She hands* USNAVI *a brown paper bag. He looks inside.*)

USNAVI

ABUELA, I'VE NEVER SEEN—

USNAVI/ABUELA CLAUDIA

THIS MUCH MONEY IN MY LIFE!

(BENNY *finds* NINA *on the street.*)

BENNY

NINA, THERE YOU ARE!

NINA

I'VE GOTTA GO!

BENNY

I'LL GET YOU OUT OF HERE TONIGHT!

NINA

I DON'T NEED ANYTHING!
TONIGHT, I CAN FIND MY WAY HOME—

BENNY

THEN FIND YOUR WAY HOME!

(NINA *stops.*)

NINA

WITHOUT YOU—

NINA/BENNY

WITHOUT YOU—

(*She runs away from him.*)

GROUP 1 (USNAVI/KEVIN/SONNY/OTHERS)

LOOK AT THE FIREWORKS!

GROUP 2 (PIRAGUA GUY/DANIELA/CARLA/OTHERS)

LOOK AT THE FIREWORKS!

GROUP 1

LOOK AT THE FIREWORKS!

GROUP 2

LOOK AT THE FIREWORKS!

ALL

LIGHT UP THE NIGHT SKY!

CARLA/DANIELA/PIRAGUA GUY/TWO MEN

LIGHT UP THE NIGHT SKY!

ALL

EN WASHINGTON—
LOOK AT THE FIREWORKS!
LOOK AT THE FIREWORKS!

VANESSA/ABUELA CLAUDIA/USNAVI/OTHERS

LIGHT UP THE NIGHT SKY—

GRAFFITI PETE/THREE WOMEN/THREE MEN

LIGHT UP THE NIGHT SKY—

(BENNY *finds* NINA, *grabs her. They kiss, illuminated by fireworks.*)

ALL

EN WASHINGTON HEIGHTS!

END OF ACT ONE

ACT 2
SCENE 1

(*Sunday morning. The sky is still dark, the power is still out. We hear the sound of a coqui, welcoming the morning. Slowly, the sounds of approaching dawn. NINA and BENNY appear, arm in arm, on his fire escape.*)

"Sunrise"

NINA

ARE YOU READY TO TRY AGAIN?

BENNY

I THINK I'M READY.

NINA

Okay. Here we go.
ESQUINA.

BENNY

CORNER.

NINA

TIENDA.

BENNY

STORE.

NINA

BOMBILLA.

BENNY

LIGHT BULB—

NINA

You're sure?

BENNY

I'm sure.

NINA

THREE OUT OF THREE, YOU DID ALRIGHT!

BENNY

TEACH ME A LITTLE MORE . . .

NINA

CALOR.

BENNY

HEAT.

NINA

ANOCHE.

BENNY

LAST NIGHT.

NINA

DOLOR.

BENNY

PAIN.

NINA

THAT'S RIGHT.

LLÁMAME.

BENNY

CALL ME.

NINA

AZUL.

BENNY

BLUE.

NINA

ÁMAME.

BENNY

LOVE ME.

NINA

PERHAPS I DO.

BENNY

WELL, HOW DO YOU SAY KISS ME?

NINA

BÉSAME.

BENNY

AND HOW DO YOU SAY HOLD ME?

NINA

ABRÁZAME.
AL AMANECER. AT SUNRISE.

NINA/BENNY

ANYTHING AT ALL CAN HAPPEN JUST BEFORE THE SUNRISE.

NINA

AL AMANECER.

ACT 2   97

BENNY

AL AMANECER.

(*A little more light shines, revealing the street below.* USNAVI*'s window has been smashed. There is trash all around.*)

SONNY

SUNRISE.

CARLA

SUNRISE.

VANESSA

SUNRISE.

DANIELA

SUNRISE.

PIRAGUA GUY/THREE MEN
SIGUE ANDANDO EL CAMINO   **CARLA**
POR TODA SU VIDA.   SUNRISE.

                                              VANESSA
                                          SUNRISE.

                                              DANIELA
                                          SUNRISE.

                                              ALL THREE + SONNY
                                          SUNRISE.

RESPIRA.

KEVIN

NINA—

BENNY

I DON'T KNOW.

NINA

YO NO SÉ.

BENNY

WHAT TO DO,

NINA

QUE HACER,

BENNY

NOW THAT I'VE FOUND YOU.

NINA

AHORA QUE TE ENCONTRÉ.

BENNY

WHAT WILL HE SAY?

NINA

QUE DIRÁ?

BENNY

WHEN HE SEES ME AROUND YOU?
SO HOW DO YOU SAY HELP ME?

NINA

AYÚDAME.

BENNY

AND HOW DO YOU SAY PROMISE ME?

NINA

PROMÉTEME.

NINA/BENNY

PROMISE ME YOU'LL STAY BEYOND THE SUNRISE.
I DON'T CARE AT ALL WHAT PEOPLE SAY BEYOND THE SUNRISE.

NINA

PROMISE ME YOU'LL STAY.

BENNY

I'LL STAY.

SONNY/PIRAGUA GUY/MAN

SUNRISE.

CARLA/VANESSA/WOMAN

SUNRISE.

DANIELA/TWO WOMEN

SUNRISE.

USNAVI/GRAFFITI PETE/THREE MEN

SUNRISE.

BENNY

AND HOW DO YOU SAY KISS ME?

NINA

BÉSAME . . .

BENNY	**SONNY/PIRAGUA GUY/MAN**
BÉSAME . . .	SUNRISE

CARLA/VANESSA/WOMAN

SUNRISE

DANIELA/TWO WOMEN

SUNRISE

**USNAVI/GRAFFITI PETE/
THREE MEN**

SUNRISE

BENNY

OH, AND HOW DO YOU SAY ALWAYS?

NINA

PARA SIEMPRE . . .

BENNY

PARA SIEMPRE . . .

USNAVI/VANESSA/DANIELA/OTHERS

AL AMANECER

NINA

AL AMANECER

BENNY

AL AMANECER

ENSEMBLE

AL AMANECER

NINA/BENNY

I WILL BE THERE.
AL AMANECER.

SCENE 2

(USNAVI *outside the bodega. The awning is slashed, the window is broken. Neighbors stand by, looking at the damage.*)

DANIELA

Whoever did that, I'm gonna put a jinx on their head.

CARLA

'Dito, Usnavi, let us help you clean up.

USNAVI

Thanks but I'd like to be alone with my broken window.

(DANIELA *and* CARLA *exit into the salon.* USNAVI *finds a ripped-up dollar on the floor, picks it up.*)

(SONNY *enters from the bodega.*)

SONNY

I got most of the glass up.

USNAVI

Recognize this?

SONNY

Oh man, the bodega's first customer . . . ?

USNAVI

First dollar my dad made here. (*He puts it down.*) Bueno, take whatever batteries and candles we have to the church on Audubon.

SONNY

You don't need backup?

USNAVI

For what?

SONNY

For your soul. Dr. Phil said denial is the first stage of grief.

USNAVI

It's a stolen register, a ripped-up awning, it's just things.

(VANESSA *enters.*)

VANESSA

I heard.

USNAVI

I still got a gas range, can I make you some coffee?

VANESSA

You got actual stuff to deal with.

USNAVI

Listen, about last night, Sonny was calling, Abuela was alone . . .

VANESSA

My phone didn't ring once all night. No one wanted to know if I was okay.

USNAVI

I meant to call.

VANESSA

Sorry about your bodega.

(*She exits.* GRAFFITI PETE *enters.*)

GRAFFITI PETE

Yo, Sonny, come check out my new wall! I painted that shit by candlelight!

SONNY

Shh, the man's having female troubles.

GRAFFITI PETE

My bad . . .

USNAVI

(*To* GRAFFITI PETE.) You got a new canvas. Tag up the whole store, have a blast.

(*He exits. Lights shift to* CAMILA *on the Rosario fire escape.* KEVIN
enters.)

KEVIN

Thank God. Where have you been?

CAMILA

Waiting here since three in the morning for you and Nina.

KEVIN

You should check your messages, I've been combing the streets all night looking for the two of you!

CAMILA

My phone died. She went dancing. I tried to find her after the blackout.

KEVIN

She followed your lead. She walked out the door, same as you!

CAMILA

Pero, carajo, who opened that door?

KEVIN

Camila!

CAMILA

Later, Papi. Right now we find our daughter.

SCENE 3

(Interior of USNAVI *and* ABUELA's *apartment.* USNAVI *enters.* ABUELA *is there with the bag of money.)*

"Hundreds of Stories"

USNAVI

ABUELA.

ABUELA CLAUDIA

ARE YOU OKAY?

ABUELA CLAUDIA/USNAVI

PACIENCIA Y FE!
PACIENCIA Y FE!

USNAVI

LET ME SEE IT AGAIN!

(*He looks in the bag.*)

ABUELA CLAUDIA

WE KEPT IT SAFE.

USNAVI

SO WE SURVIVED THE NIGHT.
WHAT HAPPENS TODAY?

ABUELA CLAUDIA

A THIRD FOR YOU.

USNAVI

UH-HUH, UH-HUH. UH-HUH, UH-HUH.

ABUELA CLAUDIA

A THIRD FOR ME!

USNAVI

NO PARE SIGUE SIGUE!

ABUELA CLAUDIA

THE REST FOR SONNY.
AND WITH OUR SHARE OF THE MONEY
AND WITH OUR SHARE OF THE MONEY—

DREAM OF THE SEASIDE AIR!
SEE ME BESIDE YOU THERE!
THINK OF THE HUNDREDS OF STORIES WE WILL SHARE!

YOU AND I!

USNAVI/ABUELA CLAUDIA

AYY—

ABUELA CLAUDIA

NOW YOU CAN SELL YOUR STORE!
OPEN A BAR BY THE SHORE!
I'VE TOLD YOU HUNDREDS OF STORIES
ABOUT HOME. MAKE SOME MORE.

USNAVI/ABUELA CLAUDIA

MORE—

USNAVI

YO! I KNOW JUST WHERE TO GO!
THERE'S A LITTLE BEACH NAMED PLAYA RINCÓN
WITH NO ROADS, YOU NEED A ROWBOAT OR MOTORBIKE
TO REACH THIS BEACH AND IT'S JUST A STONE'S THROW
FROM HOME.
MY FOLKS' HOME.
BEFORE I WAS BORN.
BEFORE THEY PASSED ON.
AND LEFT ME ON MY OWN, IN NEW YORK, WITH THE GROCERY STORE.
THEY WOULD TALK ABOUT HOME. I LISTENED CLOSELY FOR
THE WAY THEY WHISPERED TO EACH OTHER
'BOUT THE WARMER WINTER WEATHER.
INSEPARABLE, THEY EVEN GOT SICK TOGETHER.
BUT THEY NEVER GOT BETTER, PASSED AWAY THAT DECEMBER
AND LEFT ME WITH THESE MEMORIES LIKE DYIN' EMBERS
FROM A DREAM I CAN'T REMEMBER.
EVER SINCE THEN IT'S LIKE
ANOTHER DAY DEEPER IN DEBT WITH DIFFERENT DILEMMAS!
THE BODEGA'S A MESS, I'LL BE SEEING LESS OF VANESSA.
ABUELA, I DON'T KNOW HOW I CAN KEEP IT TOGETHER—

ABUELA CLAUDIA

REMEMBER THE STORY OF YOUR NAME?
IT WAS ENGRAVED ON A PASSING SHIP ON THE DAY YOUR FAMILY CAME.
YOUR FATHER SAID "USNAVI,

THAT'S WHAT WE'LL NAME THE BABY."

                    USNAVI
IT REALLY SAID U.S. NAVY, BUT HEY,
I WORKED WITH WHAT THEY GAVE ME, OKAY?

                ABUELA CLAUDIA
THEY'D BE SO PROUD OF YOU TODAY!

                    USNAVI
THEN BY THE END OF JULY—

                ABUELA CLAUDIA
UH-HUH, UH-HUH. UH-HUH.

                    USNAVI
OUT WHERE THE SEA MEETS THE SKY!

                ABUELA CLAUDIA
NO PARE SIGUE SIGUE!

            USNAVI/ABUELA CLAUDIA
THINK OF THE HUNDREDS OF STORIES
WE'LL CREATE.
YOU AND I!
AY—

                ABUELA CLAUDIA
WE'LL FIND YOUR ISLAND—

                    USNAVI
MY ISLAND SKY—

                ABUELA CLAUDIA
AY, FIND YOUR ISLAND—

                    USNAVI
BUT WHATEVER WE DO IT'S—

YOU AND I!

SCENE 4

(*Outside the dispatch booth.* CAMILA *sits alone.* KEVIN *enters.*)

KEVIN
I went down to the park, nothing. Any word here?

CAMILA
Mostly voicemails, half of people's phones are out . . . I got to the letter M . . .

KEVIN
Mira, alli está.

(NINA *enters.*)

NINA
Mom, Dad.

KEVIN
Start talking.

CAMILA
Where the hell have you been?

NINA
I should have called, I know.

KEVIN
Answer your mother! Where were you?

(BENNY *enters.*)

BENNY
Boss, Mrs. Rosario. Can I have a minute?

(KEVIN *shoots* NINA *a look.*)

NINA

It's okay, Dad.

KEVIN

Think very hard about what you say to me.

NINA

Just hear him out.

KEVIN

(*To himself.*) Actually, no. (*To* BENNY.) I'll say this nicely. Please stay away from my daughter.

BENNY

Sir, I've worked here since I was practically a kid. You know me.

KEVIN

Do you think you're anywhere close to her level?

BENNY

Of course not, sir. No one is.

NINA

Stop calling him "sir."

KEVIN

(*To* NINA.) You stay out of this!

NINA

Jesus, Dad . . .

KEVIN

(*To* BENNY.) I taught you how to drive. I taught you how to tie a goddamn tie!

BENNY

And now I tie the same Windsor knot around my collar as you. We're not that different.

KEVIN

You know nothing about our culture!

BENNY

This bullshit again?

CAMILA

(*Overlapping.*) Kevin, cálmate.

KEVIN

You will never be a part of this family, entiendes?

BENNY

Loud and clear.

(*He goes to exit.*)

NINA

Benny!

BENNY

Why learn the language if they still won't hear you?

(*He exits.*)

KEVIN

(*To* NINA.) Sin vergüenza! Are you trying to shame me?

NINA

Yes, Dad, that's exactly what I'm trying to do!

KEVIN

Well, you have succeeded! Congratulations, you succeed at everything—

(*Overlapping.*) Sorry I embarrass you!

"Enough"

CAMILA

Oh my God, ENOUGH!
NOW YOU LISTEN TO ME.

NINA

Mom—

CAMILA

CARAJO, I SAID ENOUGH!
I'M SICK OF ALL THIS FIGHTING!

KEVIN

Cami—

(CAMILA *makes a yapping noise in his direction.*)

CAMILA

YAPAPAPAPA!
I THINK YOU'VE SAID ENOUGH.
NOW LISTEN TO WHAT I SAY.
WHAT I SAY GOES.

PAPI, YOU'VE PUSHED US ALL AWAY!

KEVIN

I'm trying to—

CAMILA

I DON'T WANNA HEAR IT! WE MAKE DECISIONS AS A FAMILY.
AND THROWING BENNY OUT LIKE THAT?
YOU SOUND JUST LIKE YOUR FATHER!
WE BOTH KNOW WHAT A SONOFABITCH HE WAS!

YOU THINK IT ALL COMES DOWN TO YOU—

(KEVIN *goes to embrace her.*)

KEVIN

CAMI, LET'S TALK ABOUT IT—

(CAMILA *shoves him away.*)

CAMILA

NO NO NO NO NO!
NO NO NO NO NO! NO YOU DON'T!
WHEN YOU HAVE A PROBLEM YOU COME HOME.
YOU DON'T GO OFF AND MAKE MATTERS WORSE ON YOUR OWN.
ONE DAY YOU'RE GONNA COME BACK HOME
AND YOU'RE NOT GONNA FIND ME WAITING ANY MORE.

KEVIN

I'm sorry.

CAMILA

Huh. DAMN RIGHT YOU'RE SORRY.

(CAMILA *turns her attention to* NINA.)

SO YOU STAYED OUT ALL NIGHT.

NINA

Mom—

CAMILA

I'M TALKING NOW.
YOU SCARED US HALF TO DEATH. YOU KNOW THAT, RIGHT?

NINA

I'm sorry—

CAMILA

DON'T APOLOGIZE TO ME. YOU SAVE IT FOR YOUR FATHER.

NINA

What?

CAMILA

LOOK AT YOUR FATHER.
HE DOESN'T SLEEP WHEN YOU'RE GONE.
HE'S WORKED HIS WHOLE LIFE TO HELP YOU GO FARTHER.
AND HE CAN'T ADMIT WHEN HE'S WRONG.
NOW WHO DOES THAT REMIND YOU OF?
YOU TWO DESERVE EACH OTHER!
FOR MONTHS YOU'VE LIED TO US.
WHAT DID WE DO
TO MAKE YOU THINK WE WOULDN'T DO ANYTHING AND EVERYTHING FOR YOU?
WHEN YOU HAVE A PROBLEM YOU COME HOME.
YOU DON'T RUN OFF AND HIDE FROM YOUR FAMILY ALL ALONE!
YOU HEAR ME?
WHEN YOU HAVE A PROBLEM YOU COME HOME.
AS LONG AS WE'RE ALIVE, YOU'RE NEVER ON YOUR OWN.
LEAVE BENNY.
TAKE BENNY.
IT DOESN'T MAKE ANY DIFFERENCE, AS LONG AS YOU COME HOME!

KEVIN

Camila—

CAMILA

NO NO NO NO NO!
ENOUGH LYING
ENOUGH SCREAMING
I'M DONE TRYING
AND I AM LEAVING IT UP TO YOU.
IT'S UP TO YOU.
I'LL SEE YOU BOTH BACK HOME.
ENOUGH.

(CAMILA *exits.* KEVIN *exits after her.* NINA *goes to* CLAUDIA*'s stoop, knocks, exits into her apartment.*)

"Everything Is Melting (Reprise)"

DANIELA/SONNY/VANESSA/OTHERS

WHOOAA
WHOOAA!

SCENE 5

(*Later that morning. Neighbors are sitting in the sun, exhausted.*)

SONNY

My friend was trapped in the subway. They had to walk a mile in that dank, nasty tunnel. And he stepped on a rat.

GRAFFITI PETE

Aw, hells no!

(DANIELA *enters.*)

DANIELA

Okay, people, I got through to Con Edison! They said it would be at least twenty-four hours—

PIRAGUA GUY

(*Overlapping.*) No frickin' joda.

VANESSA

(*Overlapping.*) Are you serious?

GRAFFITI PETE

(*Overlapping.*) That's some bullshit.

DANIELA

We can complain or we can get organized.

GRAFFITI PETE/VANESSA/PIRAGUA GUY

Complain!

DANIELA

(*To* GRAFFITI PETE.) Here. It's called a broom. (*To* VANESSA.) It's the Fourth of July, show some fucking spirit!

(*Neighbors reluctantly clean.*)

VANESSA

I'm catching a bus downtown for lunch. Who's hungry?

SONNY

They stopped all the buses. No traffic lights.

VANESSA

This is like Gilligan's Ghetto Island.

DANIELA

Graffiti Petie, pónla musica.

GRAFFITI PETE

I'm out of batteries.

SONNY

The dispatch has a generator.

GRAFFITI PETE

Ain't nobody there.

CARLA

Well, can't you open a hydrant?

GRAFFITI PETE

The popo's took my monkey wrench.

DANIELA
Play nice.

SONNY
My sneakers are stuck to the damn street.

CARLA
My fingernails are slipping off in the heat!

"Carnaval Del Barrio"

DANIELA
HEY . . . HEY . . .
WHAT'S THIS TONTERÍA THAT I'M SEEING ON THE STREET?
I NEVER THOUGHT I'D SEE THE DAY.
SINCE WHEN ARE LATIN PEOPLE SCARED OF HEAT?
WHEN I WAS A LITTLE GIRL
GROWING UP IN THE HILLS OF VEGA ALTA
MY FAVORITE TIME OF YEAR WAS CHRISTMASTIME!
ASK ME WHY!

CARLA
Why?

DANIELA
THERE WASN'T AN OUNCE OF SNOW
BUT OH, THE COQUITO WOULD FLOW
AS WE SANG THE AGUINALDO,
THE CARNAVAL WOULD BEGIN TO GROW!
BUSINESS IS CLOSED, AND WE'RE ABOUT TO GO . . .
LET'S HAVE A CARNAVAL DEL BARRIO!

PIRAGUA GUY
Wepa!

(PIRAGUA GUY *begins to scrape a slow beat.* DANIELA *begins slowly.*)

DANIELA

CARNAVAL DEL BARRIO!
CARNAVAL DEL BARRIO!
CARNAVAL—

(SONNY *joins her effort.*)

PIRAGUA GUY

CARNAVAL!

DANIELA

DEL BARRIO—

PIRAGUA GUY

BARRIO!

DANIELA

CARNAVAL—

SONNY/PIRAGUA GUY

CARNAVAL!

DANIELA

DEL BARRIO—

SONNY/PIRAGUA GUY

BARRIO!

DANIELA

WE DON'T NEED ELECTRICIDAD!
GET OFF YOUR BUTT, AVANZA!
SACA LA MARACA, BRING YOUR TAMBOURINE!
COME AND JOIN THE PARRANDA!

PIRAGUA GUY

WEPA!

(*The community gets into it.*)

DANIELA/TWO MEN/WOMAN

CARNAVAL—

DEL BARRIO!

DANIELA/PIRAGUA GUY/
TWO MEN/TWO WOMEN

CARNAVAL—

DEL BARRIO!

SONNY/PIRAGUA GUY/
DANIELA/OTHERS

CARNAVAL—

DEL BARRIO!

CARNAVAL—

DEL BARRIO!

SONNY/MAN/WOMAN

CARNAVAL!

BARRIO!

SONNY/TWO MEN/TWO WOMEN

CARNAVAL!

BARRIO!

GRAFFITI PETE/TWO MEN/THREE
WOMEN

CARNAVAL!

BARRIO!

CARNAVAL!

BARRIO!

CARLA

OOH, ME, ME, ME, DANI, I HAVE A QUESTION.
I DON'T KNOW WHAT YOU'RE CANTANDO.

DANIELA

JUST MAKE IT UP AS YOU GO!
WE ARE IMPROVISANDO!
LAI LE LO LAI LO LE LO LAI,
YOU CAN SING ANYTHING!
CARLA, WHATEVER POPS INTO YOUR HEAD,
JUST SO LONG AS YOU SING!

CARLA

MY MOM IS DOMINICAN-CUBAN, MY DAD IS FROM CHILE AND P.R., WHICH
MEANS:
I'M CHILE-DOMINI-CURICAN, BUT I ALWAYS SAY I'M FROM QUEENS!

PIRAGUA GUY

WEPAAA!

SONNY/PIRAGUA GUY/DANIELA/ OTHERS	GRAFFITI PETE/TWO MEN/THREE WOMEN
CARNAVAL—	
	CARNAVAL!
DEL BARRIO!	
	BARRIO!
CARNAVAL—	
	CARNAVAL!
DEL BARRIO!	
	BARRIO!

(VANESSA *takes center stage.*)

VANESSA

YO! WHY IS EVERYONE SO HAPPY?
WE'RE SWEATING AND WE HAVE NO POWER!
I'VE GOTTA GET OUT OF HERE SOON,
THIS BLOCK'S GETTING WORSE BY THE HOUR!
YOU CAN'T EVEN GO TO A CLUB WITH A FRIEND
WITHOUT HAVING SOMEBODY SHOVE YOU!

DANIELA

AY, POR FAVOR,
VANESSA, DON'T PRETEND THAT USNAVI'S YOUR FRIEND, WE ALL KNOW
THAT HE LOVE YOU!

COMPANY

OHHHH!

CARLA

WOW, NOW THAT YOU MENTION THAT SEXUAL TENSION, IT'S EASY TO SEE!

VANESSA

YO, THIS IS BOGUS!

DANIELA
HAVEN'T YOU NOTICED YOU GET ALL YOUR COFFEE FOR FREE?

SONNY/PIRAGUA GUY/DANIELA/ OTHERS
CARNAVAL—

DEL BARRIO!

CARNAVAL—

DEL BARRIO!

GRAFFITI PETE/TWO MEN/THREE WOMEN
CARNAVAL!

BARRIO!

CARNAVAL!

BARRIO!

MAN
HERE COMES USNAVI!

(USNAVI *enters from his apartment.*)

USNAVI
YO, YO, YO, Y-Y-YO-YO
NOW, NOW, EVERYONE GATHER 'ROUND, SIT
DOWN, LISTEN, I GOT AN ANNOUNCEMENT!
WOW, IT INVOLVES LARGE AMOUNTS, IT'S
SOMEWHERE IN THE RANGE OF NINETY-SIX THOUSAND
ATENCIÓN, I'M CLOSIN' SHOP!
SONNY, GRAB EVERYBODY A SODA POP!
YO, GRAB A BOTTLE, KISS IT UP TO GOD,
'CUZ ABUELA CLAUDIA JUST WON THE LOTTO!
YEAH, ABUELA CLAUDIA WON THE LOTTO,
WE'RE BOOKIN' A FLIGHT FOR D.R. TOMORROW!

COMPANY
OH MY GAH!

(*The company hoists* USNAVI *on their shoulders and begins marching flags around the street.* SONNY *exits into* CLAUDIA'*s place with a soda bottle.*)

ALZA LA BANDERA
LA BANDERA DOMINICANA
ALZA LA BANDERA
LA BANDERA PUERTORIQUEÑA
ALZA LA BANDERA
LA BANDERA MEJICANA
ALZA LA BANDERA
LA BANDERA CUBANA

PIRAGUA GUY	**ALL**
PA'RIBBA ESA BANDERA!	HEY!
ALZALO DONDE QUIERA!	HEY!
RECUERDO DE MI TIERRA!	

PIRAGUA GUY/USNAVI	**ALL**
ME ACUERDO DE MI TIERRA!	
ESA BONITA BANDERA!	HEY!
CONTIENE MI ALMA ENTERA!	HEY!
Y CUANDO YO ME MUERA,	
ENTIÉRRAME EN MI TIERRA!	

(*Dance break!* USNAVI *is in the center, getting love from the ladies, inverse of* VANESSA's *club number moment.*)

DANIELA

EVERYTHING CHANGES TODAY

COMPANY

HEY!

DANIELA/CARLA

USNAVI'S ON HIS WAY

COMPANY

HEY!

DANIELA/CARLA

OFF TO A BETTER PLACE

COMPANY

HEY!

DANIELA/CARLA

LOOK AT VANESSA'S FACE!

BENNY

EVERYTHING CHANGES TODAY!

COMPANY

HEY!

BENNY

GOODBYE, MR. ROSARIO—

USNAVI

OKAY!

BENNY

I'M TAKING OVER THE BARRIO!

USNAVI

YO!

USNAVI/DANIELA/CARLA

WE'RE GETTING OUT OF THE BARRIO!

DANIELA

HEY, MR. BENNY, HAVE YOU SEEN ANY HORSES TODAY?

COMPANY

HEY!

BENNY

WHAT DO YOU MEAN?

DANIELA

I HEARD YOU AND NINA WENT FOR A ROLL IN THE—

ALL

HAY! HEY! OHHHHHH!

WOMEN	**MEN**
BENNY AND NINA	BENNY AND NINA
SITTING IN A TREE	SITTING IN A TREE
K-I-S-S-I-N-G!	K-I-S-S-I-N-G!
QUE BOCHINCHE!	QUE BOCHINCHE!
NINA AND BENNY!	NINA AND BENNY!
K-I-S-S-I-N-G!	K-I-S-S-I-N-G!

SONNY	**GRAFFITI PETE/MAN**
HOLD UP, WAIT A MINUTE!	WAIT A MINUTE!
USNAVI'S LEAVIN' US FOR THE	
DOMINICAN REPUBLIC?	
AND BENNY WENT AND STOLE THE	
GIRL	
THAT I'M IN LOVE WITH?	
SHE WAS MY BABYSITTER FIRST!	HOO!
LISTEN UP, IS THIS	
WHAT Y'ALL WANT?	
WE CLOSE THIS BODEGA,	
THE NEIGHBORHOOD IS GONE!	
THEY SELLING THE DISPATCH, THEY	
CLOSING THE SALON	
AND THEY'LL NEVER TURN THE	
LIGHTS BACK ON 'CUZ—	

SONNY/VANESSA

WE ARE POWERLESS, WE ARE POWERLESS!

SONNY

BUT Y'ALL KEEP DANCIN' AND SINGIN' AND CELEBRATIN'
BUT IT'S GETTIN' LATE AND THIS PLACE IS DISINTEGRATIN' AND—

SONNY/VANESSA

WE ARE POWERLESS, WE ARE POWERLESS!

USNAVI

ALRIGHT, WE'RE POWERLESS, SO LIGHT UP A CANDLE!
THERE'S NOTHING GOING ON HERE THAT WE CAN'T HANDLE!

SONNY

YOU DON'T UNDERSTAND, I'M NOT TRYING TO BE FUNNY!

USNAVI

WE'RE GONNA GIVE A THIRD OF THE MONEY TO YOU, SONNY!

SONNY

WHAT?

USNAVI

YEAH, YEAH . . .

SONNY

FOR REAL?

USNAVI

YES!
MAYBE YOU'RE RIGHT, SONNY. CALL IN THE CORONERS!
MAYBE WE'RE POWERLESS, A CORNER FULL OF FOREIGNERS.
MAYBE THIS NEIGHBORHOOD'S CHANGING FOREVER
MAYBE TONIGHT IS OUR LAST NIGHT TOGETHER, HOWEVER!
HOW DO YOU WANNA FACE IT?
DO YOU WANNA WASTE IT, WHEN THE END IS SO CLOSE YOU CAN TASTE IT?
YOU COULD CRY WITH YOUR HEAD IN THE SAND.
I'M A-FLY THIS FLAG THAT I GOT IN MY HAND!

PIRAGUA GUY	ALL
PA'RRIBA ESA BANDERA!	HEY!

PIRAGUA GUY/DANIELA	
ALZALO DONDE QUIERA!	HEY!

USNAVI

CAN WE RAISE OUR VOICE TONIGHT?
CAN WE MAKE A LITTLE NOISE TONIGHT?

ALL

HEY!

PIRAGUA GUY/DANIELA/CARLA	ALL
ESA BONITA BANDERA!	HEY!
CONTIENE MI ALMA ENTERA!	HEY!

USNAVI

IN FACT, CAN WE SING SO LOUD AND RAUCOUS
THEY CAN HEAR US ACROSS THE BRIDGE IN EAST SECAUCUS?

PIRAGUA GUY/SONNY/ DANIELA/OTHERS	BENNY/GRAFFITI PETE/MAN/TWO WOMEN
PA'RRIBA ESA BANDERA! ALZALO DONDE QUIERA!	CARNAVAL DEL BARRIO . . .

USNAVI

FROM PUERTO RICO TO SANTO DOMINGO,
WHEREVER WE GO, WE REP OUR PEOPLE AND THE BEAT GO—

PIRAGUA GUY/SONNY/DANIELA/ OTHERS	GRAFFITI PETE/BENNY/FIVE WOMEN/FOUR MEN
ESA BONITA BANDERA! CONTIENE MI ALMA ENTERA!	CARNAVAL DEL BARRIO!

(USNAVI *confronts* VANESSA.)

USNAVI
VANESSA, FORGET ABOUT WHAT COULDA BEEN.
DANCE WITH ME, ONE LAST NIGHT, IN THE HOOD AGAIN.

(*A moment.*)

DANIELA/CARLA
WEPA!

(*The community explodes into a final chorus around* VANESSA *and* USNAVI, *as they slowly begin to dance.*)

ALL
CARNAVAL DEL BARRIO!
CARNAVAL DEL BARRIO!

ALL	**DANIELA**
CARNAVAL DEL BARRIO!	P'ARRIBA ESA BANDERA!
	OYE!
CARNAVAL DEL BARRIO!	Y CUANDO YO ME MUERA
	ENTIÉRRAME EN MI TIERRA!
DEL BARRIO!	DEL BARRIO!
ALZA LA BANDERA	
LA BANDERA DOMINICANA	
ALZA LA BANDERA	ALZA LA BANDERA!
LA BANDERA PUERTORIQUEÑA	
ALZA LA BANDERA	
LA BANDERA MEJICANA	ADIOS!

ALL
ALZA LA BANDERA
LA BANDERA
LA BANDERA
LA BANDERA
LA BANDERA

DANIELA/PIRAGUA GUY	ALL
DEL BARRIO!	ALZA LA BANDERA!

(*All cheer.*)

"Carnaval Playoff"

USNAVI/BENNY/GRAFFITI PETE/ OTHERS	
CARNAVAL— DEL BARRIO . . .	PIRAGUA GUY/CARLA/VANESSA/ OTHERS
	BARRIO!
CARNAVAL—	
	CARNAVAL!
DEL BARRIO!	
	BARRIO!
CARNAVAL—	
	CARNAVAL!
DEL BARRIO!	
	BARRIO!
CARNAVAL—	
	CARNAVAL!
DEL BARRIO!	
	BARRIO . . .
CARNAVAL—	ALZA LA BANDERA
DEL BARRIO!	LA BANDERA DOMINICANA
CARNAVAL—	ALZA LA BANDERA
DEL BARRIO!	LA BANDERA PUERTORIQUEÑA
	ALZA LA BANDERA
	LA BANDERA CUBANA . . .

(*Neighbors exit as the carnaval continues onto the next block. Suddenly* NINA *enters from* CLAUDIA'*s stoop, panicked. She runs and grabs* USNAVI, *tells him something under the noise. They exit into* CLAUDIA'*s apartment.*)

SCENE 6

(KEVIN *in the dispatch booth, at the radio.*)

"Atención"

KEVIN

ATENCIÓN. ATENCIÓN.
ROLL DOWN YOUR WINDOWS.
TURN UP YOUR RADIOS.
UN MOMENTO, POR FAVOR.

(CAMILA *enters, stands beside him.*)

ATENCIÓN. ATENCIÓN.
PLEASE DRIVE SLOW.
LET EVERYBODY KNOW
ABUELA CLAUDIA PASSED AWAY AT NOON TODAY.

SCENE 7

(*The street. Neighbors gather around* USNAVI *and* ABUELA CLAUDIA's
stoop.)

"Alabanza"

USNAVI

SHE WAS FOUND AND PRONOUNCED . . . AT THE SCENE.
SHE WAS ALREADY LYING IN BED.
THE PARAMEDICS SAID
THAT HER HEART GAVE OUT.
I MEAN, THAT'S BASICALLY WHAT THEY SAID, THEY SAID
A COMBINATION OF THE STRESS AND THE HEAT.
WHY SHE NEVER TOOK HER MEDICINE I'LL NEVER UNDERSTAND.
I'D LIKE TO THINK SHE WENT OUT IN PEACE
WITH PIECES OF BREAD CRUMBS IN HER HAND.
ABUELA CLAUDIA HAD SIMPLE PLEASURES.
SHE SANG THE PRAISES OF THINGS WE IGNORE.
GLASS COKE BOTTLES, BREAD CRUMBS, A SKY FULL OF STARS . . .
SHE CHERISHED THESE THINGS, SHE'D SAY, "ALABANZA."
ALABANZA MEANS TO RAISE THIS

THING TO GOD'S FACE
AND TO SING, QUITE LITERALLY, "PRAISE TO THIS"
WHEN SHE WAS HERE, THE PATH WAS CLEAR.
AND SHE WAS JUST HERE, SHE WAS JUST HERE . . .

NINA

ALABANZA.
ALABANZA A DOÑA CLAUDIA, SEÑOR.
ALABANZA, ALABANZA.

ALABANZA.
ALABANZA A DOÑA CLAUDIA, SEÑOR.
ALABANZA, ALABANZA.

NINA/DANIELA/CARLA

ALABANZA.
ALABANZA A DOÑA CLAUDIA, SEÑOR.

+ SONNY

ALABANZA, ALABANZA.

+ CAMILA/BENNY

ALABANZA.
ALABANZA A DOÑA CLAUDIA, SEÑOR

+ VANESSA/KEVIN

ALABANZA, ALABANZA.

NINA/DANIELA/CARLA	CAMILA/VANESSA/PIRAGUA GUY/ OTHERS
ALABANZA	ALABANZA
	ALABANZA A DOÑA CLAUDIA, SEÑOR
	+ WOMAN/GRAFFITI PETE
ALABANZA.	ALABANZA
	+ WOMAN
	ALABANZA

ENSEMBLE + WOMAN/
TWO MEN

ALABANZA

        TWO MEN
        PACIENCIA Y FE

+ MAN

ALABANZA A DOÑA   **TWO WOMEN**   **NINA**

CLAUDIA, SEÑOR   PACIENCIA Y FE   ALABANZA

ALABANZA, ALABANZA

        ALL FOUR

        ALABANZA DOÑA   PACIENCIA Y FE

        CLAUDIA,   DOÑA CLAUDIA,

        ALABANZA,

        ALABANZA   ALABANZA,

        ALABANZA

        ALL

ALABANZA,

ALABANZA

ALABANZA

        USNAVI

ALABANZA.

SCENE 8

(*Later that afternoon.* USNAVI *and* NINA *go through old boxes of* ABUELA CLAUDIA'*s things.*)

        NINA

(*Finds an old ticket.*) New York Lotto, 1978.

        USNAVI

She thought it was bad luck to throw them away.

        NINA

(*Finds a piece of paper.*) "My Abuela's Front Door" by Usnavi de la Vega! Third grade.

USNAVI

Man, I got a check minus on that thing.

NINA

Nice handwriting. "My abuela's front door is busted up. It is falling off the—" (*Shows the paper to* USNAVI.)

USNAVI

I believe that would be "hinges." Spelled with a "j."

NINA

"The doorbell don't work. Because so many people comes over to visit the doorknob be falling out." The poet laureate of 183rd Street.

USNAVI

Nina, how much is your tuition?

NINA

She asked me about it last night.

USNAVI

Abuela would want you to have some.

NINA

I have my parents, I can't take her money. But if you could spare some of these photos, my dad would appreciate it.

USNAVI

There's a bunch more inside.

"Everything I Know"

NINA

IN THIS ALBUM THERE'S A PICTURE
OF THE LADIES AT DANIELA'S.
YOU CAN TELL IT'S FROM THE NINETIES
BY THE VOLUME OF THEIR HAIR.

THERE YOU ARE. YOU'RE JUST A BABY.
THERE WE ARE ON HALLOWEEN!
IF IT HAPPENED ON THIS BLOCK, ABUELA WAS THERE.
EVERY AFTERNOON I CAME.
SHE'D MAKE SURE I DID MY HOMEWORK.
SHE COULD BARELY WRITE HER NAME,
BUT EVEN SO . . .
SHE WOULD STARE AT THE PAPER AND TELL ME,

NINA/USNAVI

"BUENO, LET'S REVIEW,

NINA

WHY DON'T YOU TELL ME EVERYTHING YOU KNOW?"

IN THIS ALBUM THERE'S A PICTURE
OF ABUELA IN HAVANA.
SHE IS HOLDING A RAG DOLL, UNSMILING,
BLACK AND WHITE.
I WONDER WHAT SHE'S THINKING.
DOES SHE KNOW THAT SHE'LL BE LEAVING
FOR THE CITY ON A COLD, DARK NIGHT?
AND ON THE DAY THEY RAN, DID SHE DREAM OF ENDLESS SUMMER?
DID HER MOTHER HAVE A PLAN?
OR DID THEY JUST GO?
DID SOMEBODY SIT HER DOWN AND SAY,
"CLAUDIA, GET READY TO LEAVE BEHIND EVERYTHING YOU KNOW."
EVERYTHING I KNOW
WHAT DO I KNOW?

USNAVI

I'll go find those photos.

NINA

IN THIS FOLDER THERE'S A PICTURE
OF MY HIGH SCHOOL GRADUATION
WITH THE PROGRAM, MINT CONDITION
AND A STAR BESIDE MY NAME.

HERE'S A PICTURE OF MY PARENTS
AS I LEFT FOR CALIFORNIA.
SHE SAVED EVERYTHING WE GAVE HER,
EVERY LITTLE SCRAP OF PAPER.
AND OUR LIVES ARE IN THESE BOXES
WHILE THE WOMAN WHO HELD US IS GONE.
BUT WE MOVE ON, WE GROW, SO . . .
HOLD TIGHT, ABUELA, IF YOU'RE UP THERE
I'LL MAKE YOU PROUD OF EVERYTHING I KNOW!
THANK YOU, FOR EVERYTHING I KNOW.

(*The Rosarios have entered.* NINA *sees them, hands them a picture.*)

KEVIN

The day I bought the business. That man took every dollar I had.

(*Hands the picture to* CAMILA.)

CAMILA

Mr. O'Hanrahan. When half this block was Irish.

KEVIN

That Polaroid is an antique.

NINA

Dad, I have to just say this first. Benny's a good person. I hope you can trust me. Mom, I've been thinking all day about what you said, what Dad did. If you two have never quit, there's no way I'm going to. I want to go back to Stanford and finish what I started.

KEVIN

Camila?

CAMILA

Yes?

KEVIN

I'm asking for your support on this.

CAMILA

So then ask.

KEVIN

Señora Rosario, are we ready to sell the business?

CAMILA

I'll never be ready. But I know it's the right time.

KEVIN

Okay. Then I'll be a mechanic again if that's what it takes.

NINA

How can I pay you back?

KEVIN

When I was nine I took some pieces of wood and made a box. I took a rag from the kitchen and an old coffee can. I walked to the plaza in Arecibo and shined shoes for a nickel. At the end of the day there was thirty-five cents in the can. Did I spend it on candy? Did I buy toys?

CAMILA

You bought shoe polish.

KEVIN

I always had a mind for investments. Nina Rosario, Bachelor of Arts. When that day comes, we'll call it even.

NINA

I love you, Dad.

SCENE 9

(DANIELA, CARLA, *and* VANESSA *enter from the salon with a few boxes.*)

"No Me Diga (Reprise)"

DANIELA
STILL NO POWER.

CARLA/VANESSA
TELL ME SOMETHING I DON'T KNOW.

VANESSA
I THINK THAT'S ALL OF THE BOXES.

CARLA/DANIELA
TELL ME SOMETHING I DON'T KNOW.

CARLA
(*Looking at the candles.*) I'm seeing double.

DANIELA
You say that every time you wear those tight jeans.

ALL
AY DIOS MIO.

DANIELA
I got a little something-something . . .

ALL
(*Sad.*) No me diga.

DANIELA
Vanessa's new address. (*Shows a piece of paper.*) A little birdie told me you needed a credit reference.

VANESSA
What do you mean?

DANIELA

I'll cosign on the apartment. But you have to invite me for a housewarming cocktail.

VANESSA

How did you get this?

DANIELA

Usnavi swore me to secrecy . . . (*To* CARLA.) What's my rule?

CARLA

She'll do anything for you, but she won't support your mother's dysfunction.

VANESSA

I know the rule, I just never thought you meant the first part of it. (*Pause.*) I'm touched. You care about me.

DANIELA

Oye, I'm just signing the paper. You're still paying the rent!

VANESSA

Thank you!

(*She exits.*)

CARLA

Feels good, doesn't it?

DANIELA

What?

CARLA

Spreading Jesus's love.

DANIELA

I never should have gotten you that "Miracle a Day" calendar.

(DANIELA *finds her keys,* CARLA *winces. A moment.*)

CARLA

This is it. Make a farewell speech.

DANIELA

It's like a Band-Aid. Rip it off quick, you don't even notice.

(DANIELA *locks the door, they exit.*)

SCENE 10

"Piragua (Reprise)"

PIRAGUA GUY

IT'S HOTTER THAN THE ISLANDS ARE TODAY.
AND MISTER SOFTEE'S TRUCK HAS BROKEN DOWN.
AND HERE COME ALL HIS CUSTOMERS MY WAY.
I TOLD YOU, I RUN THIS TOWN!

PIRAGUA, PIRAGUA,
ONE TWENTY-FIVE, PIRAGUA!
PIRAGUA, PIRAGUA,
TWO TWENTY-FIVE, PIRAGUA!

NEW BLOCK OF ICE, HIKE UP THE PRICE,
LAI LO LE LO LAI, LAI LO LE LO LAI!
BLACKOUTS ARE NICE, BLACKOUTS ARE NICE,
LO LE LO LAI,
KEEP SCRAPING BY!
PIRAGUA!

SCENE 11

(USNAVI *in the bodega.*)

USNAVI

Sonny! Don't act like you can't hear me!

(SONNY *enters.*)

SONNY

State your purpose.

USNAVI

(*Hands* SONNY *some cash.*) Here's some of that lunch money. Go buy a few pepperoni slices.

SONNY

So it all comes down to this, my severance package?

USNAVI

Money and liberty. What you always wanted. I'm freeing you. You're free.

SONNY

You think Bert would ever abandon Ernie? You think Knight Rider would be anything without Kitt? He'd be taking a bus.

(*He turns to go as* VANESSA *enters.*)

USNAVI

Papa, you watch way too much TV. Can we talk about this tomorrow?

SONNY

Fine. Bye. See ya. This is the end of an era!

(*He exits.*)

VANESSA

He's got a point.

USNAVI

How's it going?

"Champagne"

VANESSA

SO I GOT YOU A PRESENT.
I WENT DOWNTOWN TO GET IT.
DOING ANYTHING TONIGHT?

USNAVI

CLEANING.

VANESSA

YOU'RE DONE FOR THE DAY.

USNAVI

NO WAY.

VANESSA

'CUZ WE GOT A DATE.

USNAVI

OKAY—

VANESSA

BEFORE YOU BOARD THAT PLANE.
I OWE YOU A BOTTLE OF COLD CHAMPAGNE.

USNAVI

NO . . .

VANESSA

YEAH, COLD CHAMPAGNE.

USNAVI

DAMN, THE BOTTLE'S ALL SWEATY AND EVERYTHING.
YOU WENT AND GOT THIS?

VANESSA

POP THE CHAMPAGNE.

139

USNAVI

I DON'T KNOW IF WE HAVE COFFEE CUPS
OR PLASTIC CUPS, I THINK SONNY HAS THE CUPS—

VANESSA

TONIGHT, WE'RE DRINKING STRAIGHT FROM THE BOTTLE.
USNAVI?

USNAVI

YEAH?

VANESSA

DANIELA TOLD ME WHAT YOU DID FOR ME.
AND IT'S HONESTLY THE SWEETEST THING ANYONE EVER DID FOR ME.
NOW, WHAT CAN I SAY OR DO TO POSSIBLY REPAY YOU FOR YOUR
KINDNESS?

USNAVI

HOW DO YOU GET THIS GOLD SHIT OFF?

VANESSA

USNAVI!

USNAVI

YEAH!

VANESSA

BEFORE WE BOTH LEAVE TOWN!
BEFORE THE CORNER CHANGES AND THE SIGNS ARE TAKEN DOWN.
LET'S WALK AROUND THE NEIGHBORHOOD AND SAY OUR GOODBYES.
USNAVI, ARE YOU ALRIGHT?

USNAVI

I'M FINE, I'M TRYN'A OPEN THIS CHAMPAGNE.
SEE, THE TWISTY THING IS BROKEN,
BUT I'M GONNA OPEN THIS DAMN CHAMPAGNE!

VANESSA

LEMME SEE IT.

USNAVI

NO, I GOT IT!

VANESSA

YO, USNAVI, DROP THE CHAMPAGNE!

USNAVI

YOU WENT TO ALL THAT TROUBLE TO GET US A LITTLE BUBBLY—

VANESSA

AND IT'S GONNA BE OKAY.

USNAVI

I'M SORRY. IT'S BEEN A LONG DAY.

VANESSA

YOU OUGHTA STAY.

USNAVI

WHAT?

VANESSA

YOU CAN USE THAT MONEY TO FIX THIS PLACE.

USNAVI

HA HA, VERY FUNNY.

VANESSA

AND IT'S NOT LIKE SONNY'S GOT ROLE MODELS—

USNAVI

ROLE MODELS?

VANESSA

STEPPING UP TO THE PLATE—

USNAVI

YO, WHAT ARE YOU TALKING ABOUT?

VANESSA

I'M JUST SAYING, I THINK YOUR VACATION CAN WAIT!

USNAVI

VACATION? VANESSA, YOU'RE LEAVING TOO—

VANESSA

I'M GOING DOWN TO WEST FOURTH STREET, YOU CAN TAKE THE A—

USNAVI

WHAT ARE YOU TRYING TO SAY?

VANESSA

YOU'RE LEAVING THE COUNTRY, AND WE'RE NEVER GONNA SEE YOU
AGAIN—

USNAVI

WHAT ARE YOU TRYING TO SAY?

VANESSA

YOU GET EVERYONE ADDICTED TO YOUR COFFEE AND OFF YOU GO.

USNAVI

VANESSA, I DON'T KNOW WHY YOU'RE MAD AT ME.

VANESSA

I WISH I WAS MAD—

(*She kisses him.*)

I'M JUST TOO LATE.

IN THE HEIGHTS

SCENE 12

(Sunset. BENNY is at the dispatch, KEVIN enters.)

BENNY

Thanks for coming, boss.

KEVIN

You can call me Kevin. Look, if this is about Nina—

BENNY

It's about you and me.

KEVIN

She's going back in the fall.

BENNY

(Pause.) Tomorrow I'm'a start planning my own business and I can't do that until I finish this. My uniform's on the counter, here's your keys. We're all squared away. I had your back, Kevin. Now I got my own.

(KEVIN exits. BENNY approaches NINA.)

"When the Sun Goes Down"

BENNY

WHEN THE SUN GOES DOWN
YOU'RE GONNA NEED A FLASHLIGHT.
YOU'RE GONNA NEED A CANDLE—

NINA

I THINK I CAN HANDLE THAT.

BENNY

WHEN YOU LEAVE TOWN
I'M GONNA BUY YOU A CALLING CARD.

BENNY/NINA

'CUZ I AM FALLING HARD FOR YOU.

NINA

I GO BACK ON LABOR DAY.

BENNY

AND I WILL TRY TO MAKE MY WAY

BENNY/NINA

OUT WEST TO CALIFORNIA.

BENNY

SO WE'VE GOT THIS SUMMER.

NINA

AND WE'VE GOT EACH OTHER.
PERHAPS EVEN LONGER . . .

BENNY

WHEN YOU'RE ON YOUR OWN.
AND SUDDENLY WITHOUT ME
WILL YOU FORGET ABOUT ME?

NINA

I COULDN'T IF I TRIED.

BENNY

WHEN I'M ALL ALONE
AND I CLOSE MY EYES.

BENNY/NINA

THAT'S WHEN I'LL SEE YOUR FACE AGAIN.

BENNY

AND WHEN YOU'RE GONE
YOU KNOW THAT I'LL BE WAITING WHEN YOU'RE GONE.

NINA

BUT YOU'RE HERE WITH ME RIGHT NOW—

BENNY

WE'LL BE WORKING HARD, BUT
IF WE SHOULD DRIFT APART—

NINA

BENNY—

BENNY

LEMME TAKE THIS MOMENT JUST TO SAY—

NINA

NO, NO—

BENNY

YOU ARE GONNA CHANGE THE WORLD SOMEDAY—

NINA

I'LL BE THINKING OF HOME—

BENNY/NINA

AND I'LL THINK OF YOU EVERY NIGHT
AT THE SAME TIME—

BENNY

WHEN THE SUN GOES DOWN.

NINA

WHEN THE SUN GOES DOWN.

BENNY

WHEN THE SUN GOES DOWN.

SCENE 13

(*Late at night.* SONNY *and* GRAFFITI PETE *appear in a shady alleyway.*)

GRAFFITI PETE

You paged me?

SONNY

Shh. Step into my office. I just came into a little money and I got a business proposition to throw your way.

(SONNY *whispers into* GRAFFITI PETE's *ear.*)

GRAFFITI PETE

I'm feeling that.

SONNY

Is this enough for you to get started?

GRAFFITI PETE

Shit, with this much cash I can hook it up. But it'll take me all night.

SONNY

No one knows about this but you and me, you got that?

(*They shake hands.*)

SCENE 14

(*Monday morning, sunrise. The power is still out.* KEVIN *is up on a ladder, taking down the "Rosario Car Service" sign.* CAMILA *is beside him. He hands the sign down to* CAMILA. *Underneath is the glimmer of an older sign: "O'Hanrahan Car Service."*)

"Finale"

RECORDED BOLERO SINGER

NO TE VAYAS.
SI ME DEJAS.
SI TE ALEJAS DE MI . . .
SEGUIRÁS EN MIS RECUERDOS PARA SIEMPRE.
PARA SIEMPRE . . . PARA SIEMPRE . . .
PARA SIEMPRE . . . (*Continues under next rap.*)

(USNAVI *has entered and watched this. He sits on his stoop.*)

USNAVI

LIGHTS OUT ON WASHINGTON HEIGHTS, AND NOW THE CRACK OF
DAWN.
THE BLACKOUT GOES ON AND ON AND ON.
SONNY'S OUT BACK, SORTIN' THE TRASH
AS I THINK ABOUT THE PAST, WITH A SACK FULL OF CASH.
ABUELA REALLY WANTED ME UP ON A BEACH
WITH MARGARITAS IN MY REACH, AND
SOON THAT'S HOW IT'S GONNA BE.
IMAGINE ME, LEAVING TODAY
ON A SEVEN FORTY-SEVEN BOARDIN' JFK . . .

CARLA

THE HYDRANTS ARE OPEN.
COOL BREEZES BLOW.

CARLA/DANIELA

THE HYDRANTS ARE OPEN.
COOL BREEZES BLOW.

DANIELA/CARLA	**KEVIN**
THE HYDRANTS ARE OPEN. COOL BREEZES BLOW.	GOOD MORNING.
DANIELA/CARLA	**KEVIN**
THE HYDRANTS ARE OPEN. COOL BREEZES BLOW.	GOOD MORNING.
DANIELA/CARLA	**KEVIN**
THE HYDRANTS ARE OPEN. COOL BREEZES BLOW.	GOOD MORNING.

PIRAGUA GUY

PIRAGUA. PIRAGUA.
NEW BLOCK OF ICE.
PIRAGUA.
SO SWEET AND NICE.
PIRAGUA.
PIRAGUA. PIRAGUA.

PIRAGUA GUY	CAMILA
PIRAGUA. PIRAGUA.	SIEMPRE . . .
NEW BLOCK OF ICE. PIRAGUA.	SEGUIRAS EN
SO SWEET AND NICE. PIRAGUA.	MIS RECUERDOS
PIRAGUA. PIRAGUA.	PARA SIEMPRE . . .

PIRAGUA GUY	CAMILA	VANESSA
PIRAGUA. PIRAGUA.	SIEMPRE . . .	I'LL BE DOWNTOWN . . .
NEW BLOCK OF ICE.	SEGUIRAS EN	
PIRAGUA.	MIS RECUERDOS	
SO SWEET AND NICE.	PARA SIEMPRE . . .	IT WON'T BE LONG
PIRAGUA.		NOW . . .
PIRAGUA. PIRAGUA.		

(USNAVI *is out on the sidewalk.*)

USNAVI

THERE'S A BREEZE OFF THE HUDSON
AND JUST WHEN
YOU THINK YOU'RE SICK OF LIVING HERE THE MEMORY FLOODS IN.
THE MORNING LIGHT, OFF THE FIRE ESCAPES.
THE NIGHTS IN BENNETT PARK BLASTING BIG PUN TAPES.
I'M A MISS THIS PLACE, TO TELL YOU THE TRUTH.
KEVIN DISPENSIN' WISDOM FROM HIS DISPATCH BOOTH.
AND AT DAWN, VANESSA AT THE SALON, WE GOTTA MOVE ON.
BUT WHO'S GONNA NOTICE WE'RE GONE?
WHEN OUR JOB'S DONE. AS THE EVENING WINDS
DOWN TO A CRAWL, SON. CAN I EASE MY MIND
WHEN WE'RE ALL DONE? WHEN WE'VE RESIGNED.

IN THE LONG RUN, WHAT DO WE LEAVE BEHIND?
MOST OF ALL, I'LL MISS ABUELA'S WHISPERS,
DOIN' THE LOTTO PICK SIX EVERY CHRISTMAS.
IN FIVE YEARS, WHEN THIS WHOLE CITY'S RICH FOLKS AND HIPSTERS,
WHO'S GONNA MISS THIS RAGGEDY LITTLE BUSINESS?

(USNAVI *arrives at the bodega.* SONNY *and* GRAFFITI PETE *are there.*)

GRAFFITI PETE

What it do? Great sunlight this morning.

SONNY

Yo, cuz! We fixed the grate!

USNAVI

(*To* SONNY.) What did I tell you about this punk?

SONNY

You have to commission an artist while his rate is still good.

GRAFFITI PETE

The first work in my new series.

(GRAFFITI PETE *rolls down the gate. There is a huge graffiti mural of* ABUELA CLAUDIA *that says PACIENCIA Y FE. Silence.*)

GRAFFITI PETE

He hates it.

SONNY

Shh. He's forming an artistic opinion.

(*The beat crescendos back in.*)

USNAVI

YOU DID THIS LAST NIGHT?

GRAFFITI PETE

YEAH.

USNAVI

THERE GOES MY FLIGHT.

SONNY

WHAT?

USNAVI

GRAFFITI PETE, YOU'RE GONNA NEED SOME NEW CANS!
HERE'S SOME MONEY, FINISH UP, THERE'S BEEN A SLIGHT CHANGE OF
PLANS!

GRAFFITI PETE

NICE!

USNAVI

LISTEN UP, GUYS, YOU GOT A JOB, I'M NOT PLAYIN'.
YOU GOTTA GO NOW, TELL THE WHOLE BLOCK I'M STAYIN'!
WELL, GO AHEAD, TELL EVERYONE WE KNOW!

(GRAFFITI PETE *and* SONNY *run off.*)

SONNY—

(USNAVI *starts to say something, but gets choked up, motions to his own
heart.*)

ALRIGHT, GO!

(SONNY *runs off.*)

YEAH, I'M A STREETLIGHT
CHILLIN' IN THE HEAT!
I ILLUMINATE THE STORIES OF THE PEOPLE IN THE STREET.
SOME HAVE HAPPY ENDINGS.
SOME ARE BITTERSWEET.

BUT I KNOW THEM ALL AND THAT'S WHAT MAKES MY LIFE COMPLETE.

(NINA *enters, sees the mural.*)

NINA
WE'RE HOME—

USNAVI
AND IF NOT ME, WHO KEEPS OUR LEGACIES?
WHO'S GONNA KEEP THE COFFEE SWEET WITH SECRET RECIPES?
ABUELA, REST IN PEACE, YOU LIVE IN MY MEMORIES,
BUT SONNY'S GOTTA EAT, AND THIS CORNER IS MY DESTINY.

SONNY/NINA/CARLA/DANIELA
WE'RE HOME—

USNAVI
BRINGS OUT THE BEST IN ME, WE PASS A TEST AND WE
KEEP PRESSIN' AND YES INDEED, YOU KNOW I'LL NEVER LEAVE.
IF YOU CLOSE YOUR EYES, THAT HYDRANT IS A BEACH.
THAT SIREN IS A BREEZE, THAT FIRE ESCAPE'S A LEAF ON A PALM TREE.

SONNY/DANIELA/NINA/OTHERS
WE'RE HOME—

USNAVI
ABUELA, I'M SORRY,
BUT I AIN'T GOIN' BACK BECAUSE I'M TELLING YOUR STORY!
AND I CAN SAY GOODBYE TO YOU SMILIN', I FOUND MY ISLAND
I'VE BEEN ON IT THIS WHOLE TIME.
I'M HOME!

GROUP 1 (NINA/CAMILA/SONNY/ OTHERS)	GROUP 2 (VANESSA/GRAFFITI PETE/ WOMEN/MEN)
WE'RE HOME—	THE HYDRANTS ARE OPEN, COOL BREEZES BLOW—

USNAVI

IT'S A WONDERFUL LIFE THAT I'VE KNOWN—
MERRY CHRISTMAS, YOU OL' BUILDING AND LOAN!
I'M HOME!

GROUP 1	GROUP 2
WE'RE HOME—	THE HYDRANTS ARE OPEN, COOL BREEZES BLOW—

USNAVI

ABUELA, THAT AIN'T A STOOP, THAT'S YOUR THRONE—
LONG AFTER YA BIRDS HAVE ALL FLOWN,

USNAVI	GROUP 1
I'M HOME!	WE'RE HOME!
WHERE THE COFFEE'S NONSTOP	
AND I DROP THIS HIP-HOP IN MY	**ALL**
MOM-AND-POP SHOP. I'M HOME!	WE'RE HOME!
WHERE PEOPLE COME,	
PEOPLE GO,	
LET ME SHOW ALL OF THESE	
PEOPLE WHAT I KNOW, THERE'S NO	
PLACE LIKE HOME!	WE'RE HOME!
AND LET ME SET THE RECORD	
STRAIGHT!	
I'M STEPPIN' TO VANESSA,	
I'M GETTIN' A SECOND DATE!	
I'M HOME!	WE'RE HOME!
WHERE IT'S A HUNDRED IN THE	
SHADE,	
BUT WITH PATIENCE AND FAITH,	HOME!
WE REMAIN UNAFRAID,	
I'M HOME.	HOME!
YOU HEAR THAT MUSIC IN THE AIR?	
TAKE THE TRAIN TO THE TOP OF	HOME!
THE WORLD, AND I'M THERE,	
I'M HOME!	HOME!

END OF SHOW

ACT 2   153

ABOUT THE AUTHORS

LIN-MANUEL MIRANDA (Music and Lyrics; Original Concept) won the 2008 Tony Award for Best Original Score for *In The Heights*, and a 2009 Grammy Award for its Original Broadway Cast Album; the musical was a finalist for the 2009 Pulitzer Prize for Drama. Off-Broadway accolades for *In The Heights* include a Drama Desk Award (Outstanding Ensemble Performance) and nine Drama Desk nominations (including Best Music, Best Lyrics), an Obie Award (Outstanding Music and Lyrics), a Lucille Lortel Award (Best Musical), and an Outer Critics Circle Award (Best Musical). Miranda received the 2007 ASCAP Richard Rodgers New Horizons Award. He has contributed new songs to the revival of Stephen Schwartz's *Working*, collaborated with Arthur Laurents and Stephen Sondheim on Spanish translations for the 2009 Broadway revival of *West Side Story*, and collaborated with Tom Kitt and Amanda Green on music and lyrics for Broadway's *Bring It On: The Musical*. Miranda's work in TV and film include appearances in *Modern Family, House, Sesame Street, The Electric Company, The Sopranos*, the *Sex and the City* movie, and *The Odd Life of Timothy Green*. He is a co-founding member of Freestyle Love Supreme, a hip-hop comedy group that tours comedy festivals worldwide. He lives in uptown Manhattan with his wife and dog.

QUIARA ALEGRÍA HUDES (Book) is the author of the "Elliot Trilogy" of plays. The first play, *Elliot, A Soldier's Fugue*, was a 2007 Pulitzer finalist. The second, *Water by the Spoonful*, won the 2012 Pulitzer Prize for Drama. The final play, *The Happiest Song Plays Last*, premiered at Chicago's Goodman Theatre in April 2013. Hudes wrote the book for the Broadway musical *In The Heights*, which received the 2008 Tony Award for Best Musical, a Tony nomination for Best Book of a Musical, and was a 2009 Pulitzer Prize finalist. Other works include the plays *26 Miles* and *Yemaya's Belly* and the musical *Barrio Grrrl!* Hudes's honors include a United States Artists Fontanals Fellowship, the Aetna New Voices Fellowship at Hartford Stage Company, a Joyce Foundation Award, a residency at New Dramatists, and a resolution from the City of Philadelphia. Hudes sits on the Dramatists Guild Council and serves on the board of Philadelphia Young Playwrights, which produced her first play in the tenth grade. She lives in New York with her husband and daughter.

ABOUT THE AUTHORS